1
YEAR

Classworks
Literacy

Louise Gilbert

Classroom Resources

Acknowledgements

The author and publishers wish to thank the following for permission to use copyright material:

Keep your Hamster Happy by Mal Peet, reprinted by permission of Oxford University Press.

Make a Milkshake by Amanda McArthur-Christie, reprinted by permission of Oxford University Press.

'Ten Tired Tigers', reprinted by permission of HarperCollins Publishers Ltd © David Orme.

'Zoo Dream' © 1995 John Foster, first published in *Number Poems* (Oxford University Press), included by permission of the author.

'The Magic Box' © Kit Wright, included by permission of the author.

'I Like' © John Foster, first published in *Food Poems* (Oxford University Press), included by permission of the author.

'Noisy Food' © Marian Swinger, first published in *Poems about Food*, Wayland, 1999.

'Rani Sits Beside Her Door', translation by kind permission of LCP.

'Dragon Feast' © Moira Andrew, first published in *Poems about Food*, edited by Brian Moses, Wayland 1999.

'The Sound Collector', reprinted by permission of PFD on behalf of Roger McGough © 1990 by Roger McGough.

'The Clown's Last Joke' by kind permission of John Agard c/o Caroline Sheldon Literary Agency.

'Sounds Good' © Judith Nicholls 1990, originally published in *Higgledy-Humbug* by Judith Nicholls, published by Mary Glasgow Publications. Reprinted by permission of the author.

'The Three Little Pigs' from *A Ladybird 'Easy Reading' Book*, retold by Vera Southgate © Ladybird Books Ltd.,1965

The Paper Bag Princess by Robert Munsch, illustrated by Michael Martchenko © Robert Munsch, 1980, first published in 1980 by Annick Press, Ltd. Toronto, Canada M2M 1H9. Published by Little Hippo, an imprint of Scholastic Children's Books. All rights reserved.

'We're Going on a Bear Hunt', text © Michael Rosen, from *We're Going on a Bear Hunt,* illustrated by Helen Oxenbury. Reproduced by permission of Walker Books Ltd. London.

'If I had Wings' © Pie Corbett, printed by permission of the author.

'Holi, Festival of Colour' from *An Approach to Indian Music, Song and Dance* for Schools © Punitha Perinparaja, printed by permission of the author.

'Dear Zoo' by Rod Campbell © 1982, by permission of MacMillan Childrens Books Ltd.

David Higham Associates for The Bug Chant by Tony Mitton. The Bug Chant © Tony Mitten.

Cover photo © Royalty-Free/CORBIS.

Contents

Unit	Outcome	Objectives	Page
Information Books	An information book (non-chronological report) about an animal	S5 T17, T18, T19, T21, T22, T23, T24	1
Instruction Writing	A set of instructions	S2, S4, S5, S6, S7 T2, T13, T16	12
Traditional Stories	A simple traditional story	S1, S2, S4, S5 T1, T2, T4, T5, T7, T10, T14, T16	25
Simple Dictionaries	A simple dictionary for the Reception Class	S5, T20, T25	40
Stories with A Pattern	A story with a predictable, repetitive pattern rewritten by substituting key words	S1, S3, S4, S8, S9 T2, T3, T7, T8, T11	57
Stories of Fantasy Worlds	A simple fantasy story	S1, S2, S4, S5 T1, T2, T3, T5, T6, T7, T8, T12, T13, T14	72
Fairy-tale Characters	A class book of character profiles	S6, S7 T1, T3, T6, T8, T9, T15	82
Rhymes with a Pattern	A class anthology of rhymes modelled on those read	S1, S3, S5 T1, T4, T6, T8, T10	93
Lists and Captions	Lists and captions for a class display	S2, S4, S5, S6, S7 T2, T12, T14, T15	107
Recount of a Class Visit	Recount of a visit to the Post Office, using temporal connectives	S1, S2, S4, S6, S7 T17, T18, T19, T20, T21 T22	121
Poems on a Theme: Food	Poems about food written in style of poems studied	S1, S3, S5 T1, T2, T9, T10, T12, T15, T16	131
Poems from a Range of Cultures	A variety of poems, rhymes and chants based on those read	S1, S3 T2, T3, T11, T13	146
Poems with a Pattern	Poetic sentences using repetitive patterns; performance of own poems and listening to others'	S1, S3, S6, S7 T1, T2, T4, T11, T12, T16	160
Stories with Familiar Settings	A simple recount or story based on a personal experience	S1, S4, S8, S9 T1, T3, T5, T8, T9	173

Introduction

How Classworks works

What this book contains

- Chunks of text, both annotated and 'blank' for your own annotations.

- Checklists (or toolkits), planning frames, storyboards, scaffolds and other writing aids.

- Examples of modelled, supported and demonstration writing.

- Lesson ideas including key questions and plenary support.

- Marking ladders for structured self-assessment.

- Blocked unit planning with suggested texts, objectives and outcomes.

- Word-level starter ideas to complement the daily teaching of phonics, handwriting and other skills.

- There are no scripts, no worksheets and nothing you can't change to suit your needs.

How this book is organised

- There are blocked units of work (see previous page) lasting between one week and several, depending on the text type.

- Each blocked unit is organised into a series of chunks of teaching content.

- Each 'chunk' has accompanying checklists and other photocopiable resources.

- For every text we *suggest* annotations, checklists and marking ladders.

- Every unit follows the *teaching sequence for writing* found in *Developing Early Writing* and *Grammar for Writing* (DfES 2001, 2000).

- You can mix and match teaching ideas, units and checklists as you see fit.

How you can use *Classworks* with your medium-term plan

- Refer to your medium-term planning for the blocking of NLS objectives.

- Find the text-type you want to teach (or just the objectives).

- Use the contents page to locate the relevant unit.

- Familiarise yourself with the text and language features using Classworks checklists and exemplar analysis pages, and other DfES or QCA resources such as *Grammar for Writing*.

- Browse the lesson ideas and photocopiables to find what you want to use.

- You can just use the text pages ... photocopy and adapt the checklists ... use or change some of the teaching ideas ... take whatever you want and adapt it to fit your class.

Planning a blocked unit of work with Classworks

Classworks units exemplify a blocked unit approach to planning the teaching of Literacy. What follows is an outline of this method of planning and teaching, and how *Classworks* can help you

You need: *Classworks* Literacy Year 1, medium-term planning; OHT (optional).
Optional resources: your own choice of texts for extra analysis; *Grammar for Writing*.

Method

- From the medium-term planning, identify the **outcome**, **texts** and **objectives** you want to teach.

- *Classworks* units **exemplify** how some units could be planned, resourced and taught.

- Decide how to 'chunk' the text you are analysing, for example, introductory paragraph, paragraph 1, paragraph 2, closing paragraph.

- *Classworks* units give an example of **chunking** with accompanying resources and exemplar analysis. Texts for pupil analysis (labelled 'Pupil copymaster') are intended for whole-class display on OHT.

- **Whatever you think of the checklists provided, analyse the text with *your* class and build *your own* checklist for the whole text, and for each chunk.**

- Plan your blocked unit based on the following teaching sequence for writing.

- *Classworks* units outline one way of planning a **blocked unit**, with exemplifications of some days, and suggestions for teaching content on others.

Shared Reading – analysing the text – create 'checklist' or writer's toolkit	The children analyse another of that text type and add to checklist	Review checklist
Shared Writing – demonstrate application of 'checklist' to a small piece of writing	The children write independently based on your demonstration	Use examples on OHT to check against the 'checklist'

- This model is only a guideline, allowing the writing process to be scaffolded. You would want to build in opportunities for planning for writing, talking for writing, teaching explicit word-level and sentence-level objectives that would then be modelled in the shared writing, and so on. There are ideas for word-level and sentence-level starters on pages 183–4.

- Allow opportunities for the children to be familiar with the text type. This might include reading plenty of examples, drama, role play, video, and so on.

Assessment

- Make sure that 'checklists' are displayed around the room and referred to before writing and when assessing writing in the **plenary**.

- One or two children could work on an OHT, which could be the focus of the plenary.

- Use a **marking ladder** for the children to evaluate their writing. This is based on the checklist your class has built up. We give you an example of how it might look for each blocked unit. There's a blank copy on page 185.

What each page does

Text-type written large at the top, and then on every page.

What a unit based on this material might look like.

Shaded sections refer to *Classworks* ideas, white sections to suggested extra content.

Text-based outcome clearly signalled.

Objectives spelt out.

Key aspects of teaching this text type listed.

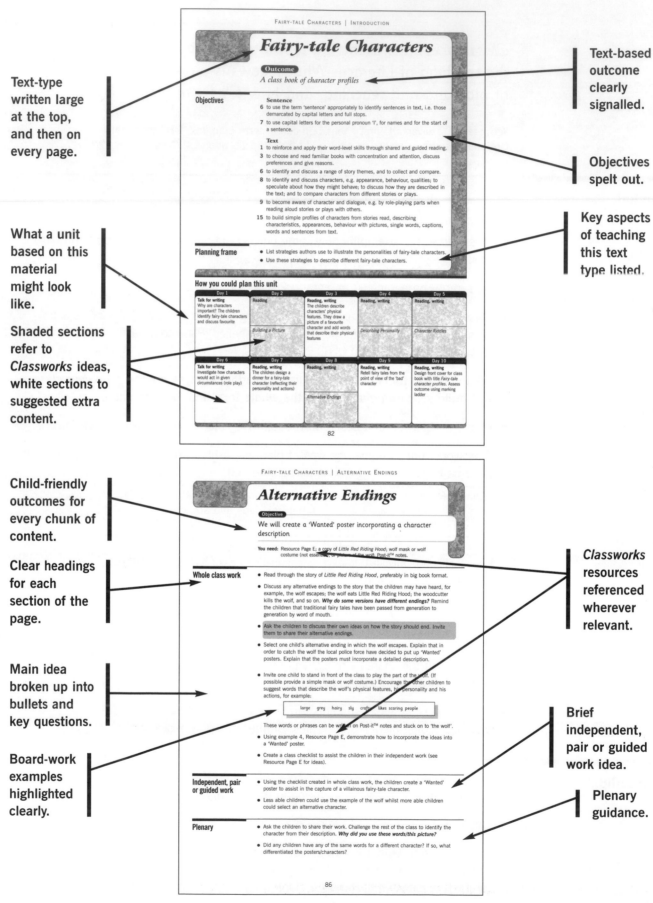

Child-friendly outcomes for every chunk of content.

Clear headings for each section of the page.

Main idea broken up into bullets and key questions.

Board-work examples highlighted clearly.

Classworks resources referenced wherever relevant.

Brief independent, pair or guided work idea.

Plenary guidance.

Information Books

Outcome

An information book (non-chronological report) about an animal

Objectives

Sentence

5 to continue demarcating sentences in writing, ending a sentence with a full stop.

Text

17 to use terms 'fiction' and 'non-fiction', noting some of their differing features.

18 to read non-fiction books and understand that the reader doesn't need to go from start to finish but selects according to what is needed.

19 to predict what a given book might be about from a brief look at the front and back covers, including blurb, title, illustration; to discuss what it might tell in advance of reading and check to see if it does.

21 to understand the purpose of contents pages and indexes and to begin to locate information by page numbers and words by initial letter.

22 to write labels for drawings and diagrams.

23 to produce extended captions.

24 to write simple questions.

Planning frame

● Distinguish between fiction and non-fiction texts.

● Discover the purpose of non-fiction texts and how to use them.

How you could plan this unit

Day 1	Day 2	Day 3	Day 4	Day 5
Reading/Talk for writing	**Reading/Writing** Create a front cover for an information book about a chosen animal. Use checklist 1 (Resource Page E)	**Writing**	**Reading/Writing** Write an introductory sentence and label a diagram of the chosen animal	**Reading/Writing**
Identifying Non-fiction		*Writing Questions*		*'Did You Know?' Boxes*

Day 6	Day 7	Day 8	Day 9	Day 10
Reading/Writing Create a checklist of things you need to look after the chosen animal	**Reading/Writing** Create a 'Remember!' box	**Reading/Writing**	**Reading/Writing** Use and create an index	**Reading/Writing** Create a back cover for the book, including a blurb. Use checklist 3 (Resource Page E). Evaluate work using the marking ladder
		Using and Creating a Contents Page		

Identifying Non-fiction

Objectives

We will understand the terms 'fiction' and 'non-fiction', and recognise some features of non-fiction books

You need: a range of fiction and non-fiction texts; a non-fiction book (preferably big) about an animal; sentences from fiction and non-fiction texts written on strips of card.

Whole class work

- Show the children the front cover of a non-fiction book about an animal.

- *What do you think the book will be about? What is it for? What kind of book is it? How might you use it?*

- Establish the idea that it is not a storybook but one that gives information. Introduce the terms 'fiction' and 'non-fiction'. Ask the children to name books they have encountered recently. Which category would they fit in to?

- Turn through the pages of the book. What do the children notice about the way that information is presented? Draw attention to, discuss, and then list the various features: contents page, index, diagrams, labels, captions, information boxes. Encourage the children to use the correct terminology. *Why do you think such features have been used?*

- Ensure the children understand that the text and pictures work together to assist the reader.

Independent, pair or guided work

- Provide each group of children with a range of fiction and non-fiction books. Encourage them to explore the various texts and sort them into non-fiction and fiction.

- The children can then use the non-fiction texts to locate the features identified during the shared session.

- Higher attaining children could go on to read the sentence strips taken from unfamiliar books, circling the sentences from non-fiction texts.

Plenary

- Ask each group to choose an example feature. *How does this feature aid the reader in obtaining information? How is the information presented?* Have any groups noticed a feature that was not identified during the shared session: the use of titles, bold headings at the top of each page, the use of photographs and so on?

- Using a collection of non-fiction and fiction books, hold up one at a time showing only the front cover. Ask the children to shout 'fiction' or 'non-fiction' appropriately. What clues on the cover enabled them to categorise the book?

- Hold up a storybook. *Would the book make sense if it was not read from beginning to end?* Establish the idea that an information text need not be read in the same manner and can be used to locate specific information.

Writing Questions

Objectives

We will write a simple question to engage a reader's interest, and use a question mark correctly

You need: a material bag containing everyday objects; flip charts or whiteboards (one between two).

Whole class work

- Hold up a bag with a variety of objects inside and invite one child secretly to select one. Encourage the rest of the class to ask questions to discover what the mystery object is. As the children raise questions, write the 'question words' they use on a flip chart or whiteboard:

> where what why when how who

Discuss the words collated.

- ***Why do you think a writer includes questions in an information box? What effect do you think it has on the reader?***

- Select an animal one of the children is using as a focus for their information text and demonstrate how to generate and write a question about that animal, for example:

> How do spiders spin webs?

- When writing, draw the children's attention to the use of a capital letter at the beginning of the sentence and the question mark, as opposed to a full stop, at the end.

- Hand out whiteboards to each pair of children. Encourage them to practise drawing a question mark, firstly in the air, and then on the whiteboard. Once confident, ask each pair to generate a question they would like to ask about the animal.

- Invite some children to share their question orally before asking them to write it on the whiteboards. Discuss examples, taking the opportunity to reinforce capitalisation, use of question marks and the spelling of question words, as well as dealing with misconceptions (misuse of question mark, capital letters, and so on).

Independent, pair or guided work

- Invite the children to write four questions, about the animal they have selected, that would engage a reader's interest, using a different question word each time.

Plenary

- Ask some children to share their work. ***Have they used capital letters at the beginning of the sentence, a question mark and a question word? Can anyone answer their questions?***

- Read out a variety of sentences. The children should draw a question mark in the air with their finger if the sentence is a question.

'Did You Know?' Boxes

Objectives

We will select information for writing a fact, and use a capital letter and full stop correctly when writing a sentence

You need: Resource Pages A and B; a range of non-fiction books about animals.

Whole class work

- Read together the example of a 'Did you know?' box (Resource Page A).

- The children join in the reading as far as possible, looking for opportunities to use a range of reading strategies to work out words that are not in their sight vocabularies.

- *What do you notice about the way the information has been organised? Why are boxes like this in the book? What type of information do they give us? What type of language has been used and why?*

- Draw attention to the clarity of the writing and why this is so important. Read the second box together. Do the features previously identified apply?

- Ask the children to discuss their chosen animal with a partner and select an appropriate fact to share with the class. Discuss some of the children's ideas and select one to write out. Make explicit links to the features identified.

> 1st sentence states a fact
>
> 2nd sentence gives advice/extra information
>
> Both have a capital letter
>
> Both have a full stop
>
> Title uses bold letters

- You may also like to make reference to strategies such as orally rehearsing a sentence before writing, counting the number of words to be written in the sentence and segmenting words into phonemes to assist spelling.

Independent, pair or guided work

- Provide the children with a variety of non-fiction books about animals. Allow the children to browse through the books in order to develop their own subject knowledge.

- Assist the children in selecting appropriate information and writing two sentences to create text for a 'Did you know?' box.

Plenary

- Select work to share with the class. Encourage the children to express why they chose particular pieces of information over others.

- *How did you know the information was appropriate? Does your first sentence state a fact and the second give further advice or information? Have you used capital letters and full stops correctly?*

Using and Creating a Contents Page

Objectives

We will understand the purpose of a contents page, and find information in a non-fiction text

You need: Resource Pages C–E; a range of non-fiction books.

Whole class work

- Remind the children that non-fiction texts don't need to be read from beginning to end but can be used to locate specific information. Ask how they might do this. Explain that a contents page helps the reader to locate the information they require.

- Share a contents page from any non-fiction big book. *What do you notice about the position of the contents page in the book?* Demonstrate how to use the contents page, then challenge the children to locate information using the page numbers.

- Share the example contents page (Resource Page C) and discuss the points indicated in the analysis (Resource Page D). Use the features identified to create a class checklist for writing contents pages (see Resource Page E, checklist 2 for ideas).

- Using your class checklist and a child's partially completed book, demonstrate how to create a contents page for that book.

Independent, pair or guided work

- Provide the children with a range of non-fiction books and encourage them to use the contents page to locate information within the text independently.

- Once confident, the children can compile the pages of their own non-fiction book, number them, and use the headings to create a contents page.

Plenary

- Ask selected children to share their contents page and demonstrate how it works. As a class, use your checklist as a marking ladder, ticking the features identified if they have been included.

- Challenge the children to locate information in an unfamiliar text or one slightly above their current reading ability. Reinforce the strategies that can be used to access the text.

(Pupil copymaster)

A 'Did you know?' box

> # Did you know?
>
> Hamsters can catch colds from humans. If you have a cold, stay away from your hamster.

> # Did you know?
>
> Your hamster's bones break easily, so don't drop it. Sit on the floor when you handle it.

from Keep Your Hamster Happy, *by Mal Peet,*
Oxford Literacy Web (OUP, 1999)

(Exemplar analysis)

Example of analysis of a 'Did you know?' box

Bold title with a capital letter and a question mark.

First sentence states a fact.

Did you know?

Hamsters can catch colds from humans. If you

Second sentence gives advice.

have a cold, stay away

from your hamster.

Both sentences begin with a capital letter and end with a full stop.

Do the features identified above apply to this example?

Did you know?

Your hamster's bones

break easily, so don't drop

it. Sit on the floor when

you handle it.

from Keep Your Hamster Happy, *by Mal Peet,*
Oxford Literacy Web (OUP, 1999)

Pupil copymaster

A contents page

Contents

from Keep Your Hamster Happy, *by Mal Peet,*
Oxford Literacy Web (OUP, 1999)

Exemplar analysis

Example of analysis of a contents page

Bold title.

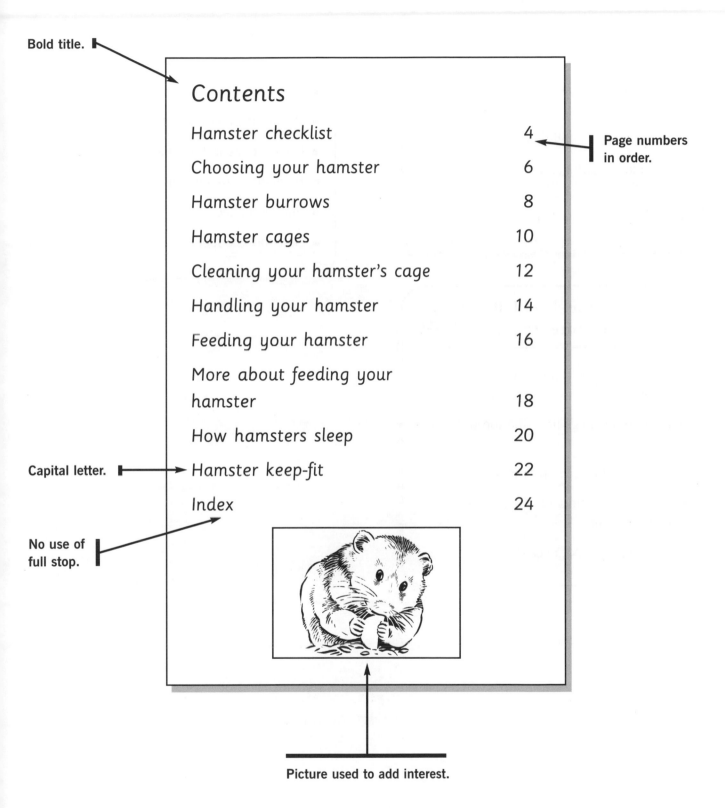

Contents

Hamster checklist	4
Choosing your hamster	6
Hamster burrows	8
Hamster cages	10
Cleaning your hamster's cage	12
Handling your hamster	14
Feeding your hamster	16
More about feeding your hamster	18
How hamsters sleep	20
Hamster keep-fit	22
Index	24

Page numbers in order.

Capital letter.

No use of full stop.

Picture used to add interest.

from Keep Your Hamster Happy, *by Mal Peet,*
Oxford Literacy Web (OUP, 1999)

Classworks Literacy Year 1 © Louise Gilbert, Nelson Thornes Ltd 2003

(Exemplar material)

Checklists for information books

Example of a checklist for creating a front page

- Use a large, clear title with a capital letter
- Use interesting lettering
- Include a clear illustration to attract attention
- Include the author's name

Example of a checklist for creating a back cover

- Blurb attracts the reader
- Picture is clear and relates to the book
- Other books in the series are detailed
- Publisher's name is included
- Price is added
- Barcode is added

Example of a checklist for creating a contents page

- Use a large, bold heading with a capital letter
- Include headings from the top of each page
- List page numbers in order
- Use capital letters for the first letter of each heading
- Full stops are not necessary

Classworks Literacy Year 1 © Louise Gilbert, Nelson Thornes Ltd 2003

(**Marking ladder**)

Name: _____

Pupil	Objective	Teacher
	My front page is clear (the reader can predict content from the cover).	
	I have used questions to engage the reader.	
	My labels and diagrams are clear.	
	I have used full stops and capital letters.	
	My sentences make sense.	
	The information selected is appropriate.	
	The information can be found using the contents page and index.	
	What could I do to improve my book next time?	

Instruction Writing

Outcome

A set of instructions

Objectives

Sentence

2 to use awareness of the grammar of a sentence to decipher new or unfamiliar words, e.g. predict text from the grammar, read on, leave a gap and reread.

4 to write captions and simple sentences, and to reread, recognising whether or not they make sense, e.g. missing words, wrong word order.

5 to recognise full stops and capital letters when reading, and name them correctly.

6 to begin using the term 'sentence' to identify sentences in text.

7 [be taught] that a line of writing is not necessarily the same as a sentence.

Text

2 to use phonological, contextual, grammatical and graphic knowledge to work out, predict and check the meanings of unfamiliar words and to make sense of what they read.

13 to read and follow simple instructions.

16 to write and draw simple instructions and labels for everyday classroom use.

Planning frame

- Write simple, clear instructions.
- Understand the importance of chronological order.

How you could plan this unit

Day 1	Day 2	Day 3	Day 4	Day 5
Talk for writing Giving verbal instructions	**Talk for writing**	**Reading**	**Writing**	**Writing** Writing instructions (continuation of Day 4)
	Making a Sandwich	*Making a Hedgehog*	*Making Something New*	

Day 6	Day 7	Day 8	Day 9	Day 10
Talk for writing/Writing The children make a drink, writing notes to recall sequence/measures	**Reading/Writing**	**Writing** Writing instructions and end statement (continuation of Day 7)	**Reading/Writing** Redrafting work using IT	**Reading/Writing** Self-assessment of work using marking ladder
	Making a Milkshake			

Making a Sandwich

Objective

We will understand why instructions must be clear and correctly ordered

You need: Resource Page A; equipment and ingredients for making a sandwich (plate, knife, jam, bread, margarine).

Whole class work

- Explain that you want to make a sandwich for your lunch. Using a knife, begin to spread margarine on to the plate. Hopefully one of the children will interrupt you at this point! Explaining that you have forgotten the order in which to make a sandwich, invite the classroom assistant to give you instructions on how to make one. *(Brief your classroom assistant on this before the lesson.)*

- In order to demonstrate what happens when instructions are unclear and given in the wrong sequence the classroom assistant should give you vague and jumbled instructions – with comical results! For example, 'Put the jam on the bread' – you could put the jam on the edge of the bread or on the crust.

- Explain that to make instructions easy to follow, they need to be clear and in the correct order.

- Invite one child to come to the front of the class and begin to make the sandwich correctly. Once they have put the margarine on the bread, ask them to stop. Encourage another member of the group to recount the first step, for example, 'Jessica got some margarine and put it on to the bread.'

- Explain that when we give instructions, in order to make them clear, we give an order such as:

> Spread the margarine on the bread!

- Get the children to wag their finger at the same time as giving an order.

- Ensure the children understand that processes, like making a sandwich, can be broken down into a sequence of actions or steps. Continue through the steps of making a sandwich, pausing after each, so that the children can change the description of what they did into a clear instruction using the imperative.

Independent, pair or guided work

- Give the children a set of pictures to sequence, detailing the various stages of making a sandwich (Resource Page A). Encourage the children to tell their response partner what instruction might accompany each picture. The partners can then jumble their sequencing cards and discuss what would have happened had the instructions been followed out of sequence.

- Lower attaining children should repeat part of the main activity. In pairs, one child instructs the other on how to make a sandwich step by step, using the imperative. The partner follows the instructions using the ingredients correctly.

Plenary

- Invite the children to give the class one clear instruction, such as 'Everyone stand up.' Once the children are confident, this may be extended to giving two or more instructions together, for example, 'Stand up, turn around and then sit down.' Ensure that the children use the imperative.

Making a Hedgehog

Objectives

We will read and follow a set of simple instructions, and work out the meanings of unfamiliar words

You need: Resource Pages B, C and G; plasticine; beads; spaghetti.

Whole class work

- Explain to the children that, having practised giving and sequencing instructions, in today's lesson they are going to read and follow a set of instructions.

- Brainstorm all the places that the children have seen instructions.

- Give the children copies of 'How to make a hedgehog' (Resource Page B). Allow them a moment to take in all the visual information. Using Resource Page C, discuss the general features associated with a set of instructions and make explicit how each feature assists the reader. Ensure that the children understand how the illustrations and text work together.

- Enter the features identified into a class checklist for a simple set of instructions (see Resource Page G for ideas).

- Read through the shared text. Encourage the children to join in the reading as far as possible and look for opportunities to make explicit a range of reading strategies. Ensure that they recognise the importance of reading the instructions in the correct order using the numbered boxes to assist them.

- At the end of the text ask the children what they think the word 'quills' means. Demonstrate how to work out what an unfamiliar word means using the context and the illustrations.

Independent, pair or guided work

- Encourage the children to read through and follow the instructions to create the hedgehog using plasticine, beads and spaghetti.

Plenary

- Referring back to the class checklist created during the shared session ask individual children to explain how the identified features assisted them in reading and following the instructions. *Which features did you find particularly useful and why?*

14

Making Something New

Objective

We will write a set of simple instructions

You need: Resource Pages B–D and G; plasticine; beads; spaghetti.

Whole class work

- Go over the instructions for making a hedgehog (Resource Page B). Explain to the children that today they will be making their own plasticine animal and will learn how to write a set of instructions to accompany it.

- Encourage the children to recall the general features associated with a set of instructions (layout, use of pictures, and so on), then explain that this session will focus on the writing.

- Point out that the title states what the instructions are about and the 'What you need' box details materials in the order they will be required (see Resource Page C).

- Draw attention to the four instruction boxes and reread as a class. Ask the children to discuss with response partners what they notice about the way the text is written, and feed back ideas.

- Ensure that the following features are discussed:
  - The sentences are short and clear to avoid the reader becoming muddled.
  - The sentences use the imperative (giving an order).
  - The instructions are in chronological order (the order in which they must happen – sequenced steps to achieve a goal).
  - Describing words (adjectives and adverbs) are only used when necessary, for example, the word 'little' in box 2.

- Compile the ideas into a class checklist for the children to use when writing (see Resource Page G for ideas).

- Using the plasticine, beads and spaghetti, make an animal, for example, an elephant, breaking the process down into four simple steps:

- Using an enlarged version of Resource Page D as a writing frame and referring to the class checklist, demonstrate how to write an instruction for each of the four steps.

> 1 Roll a ball for the body.
>
> 2 Roll a smaller ball for the head.
>
> 3 Add four legs.
>
> 4 Add a trunk.   .

Independent, pair or guided work

- The children make a simple animal using the materials provided.

- Once the task is completed, the children use the writing frame (Resource Page D) to write a set of accompanying instructions.

Plenary

- Select one child's set of instructions. Read through the instructions and follow to make the animal. Making reference to the features identified in the class checklist, discuss how easy the instructions were to follow. Prompt the children to identify elements of the writing that could have been made clearer.

Making a Milkshake

Objectives

We will write beginning and end statements for a set of instructions, and use language to signal chronological order

You need: Resource Pages E–G; whiteboards and pens (one between two).

Whole class work

- Using your class checklists, remind the children of the features necessary for a clear set of instructions. Explain that today's lesson will focus on identifying and using features that will improve the quality of their instruction writing.

- Read through *How to make a milkshake* (Resource Page E). Remind the children that it is important that instructions are given in sequence. As this text does not use numbers to identify the sequence, ask the children to identify the words within the text that have been used to signal chronological order (see Resource Page F).

- Write a list of words that could be used to signal chronological order:

> first   next   then   after   finally

Enter these words into a class checklist for improving instruction writing (see Resource Page G for ideas).

- Draw the children's attention to the last instruction – 'Drink'. Explain that although this is an instruction, it also acts as an end statement which wraps up the writing. Explain that end statements often evaluate how useful or fun an activity will be.

- Explain that as well as end statements, sets of instructions often include a statement at the beginning to tantalise the reader. As a class, devise a beginning statement for 'How to make a milkshake', for example:

> Have you ever wanted to make a delicious milkshake?
>
> You could make this tasty milkshake in just five easy steps.
>
> Surprise your friends with this mouth-watering milkshake.

- Ask the children to write a beginning statement for the drink they made in the previous lesson, using whiteboards. Share successful examples.

- Add beginning and end statements to the class checklist for improving instruction writing.

Independent, pair or guided work

- Encourage the children to write the first two instructions for making their drink. Prompt them to incorporate language to signal chronology, without using numbers.

- Final instructions and the end statement can be completed in the next lesson.

Plenary

- Ask selected children to share their beginning statement and their first instructions. Discuss the language they have chosen to tantalise the reader in their beginning statement. *Has anyone used alliteration, made good use of adjectives, or incorporated the use of a question?*

16

(**Pupil copymaster**)

Sequence cards

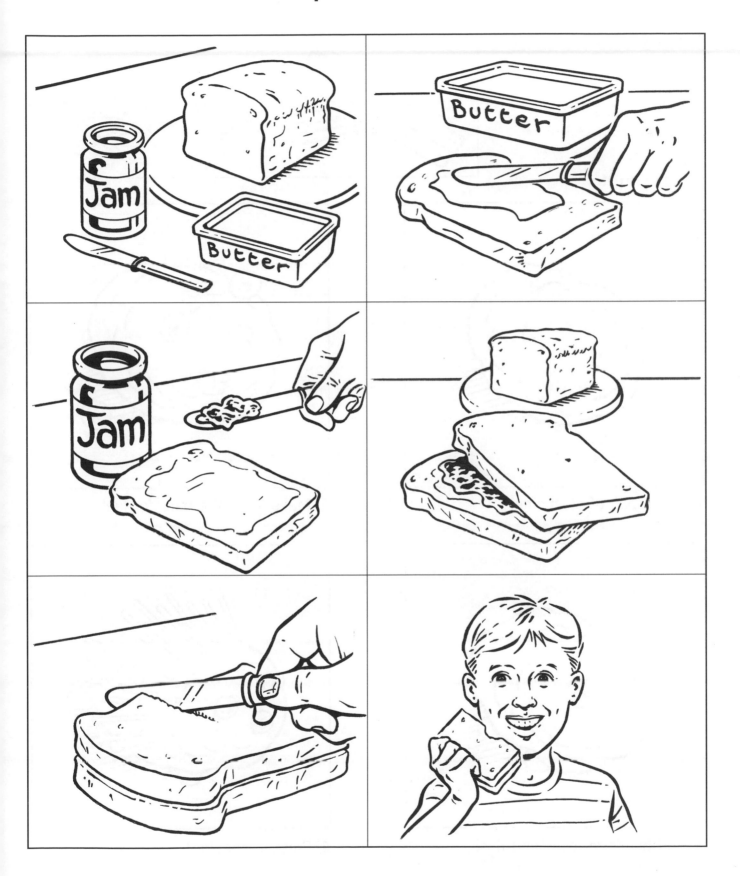

(Pupil copymaster)

How to make a hedgehog

What you need

Plasticine
Beads
Spaghetti

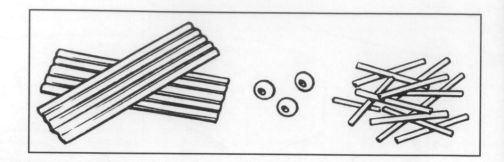

What you do

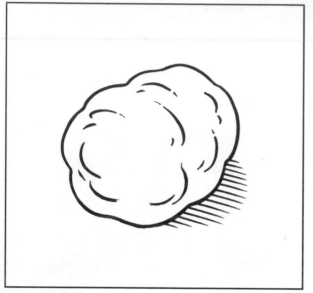

1 Roll a ball of plasticine.

2 Make four little balls for feet.

3 Add beads for eyes and nose.

4 Press in spaghetti to make quills.

from Ginn Password English

(Exemplar analysis)

Example of analysis of *How to make a hedgehog*

Title explains what the instructions are about – what is to be achieved.

Materials and ingredients are listed in order.

Diagrams, illustration and text work together.

Numbers signal order.

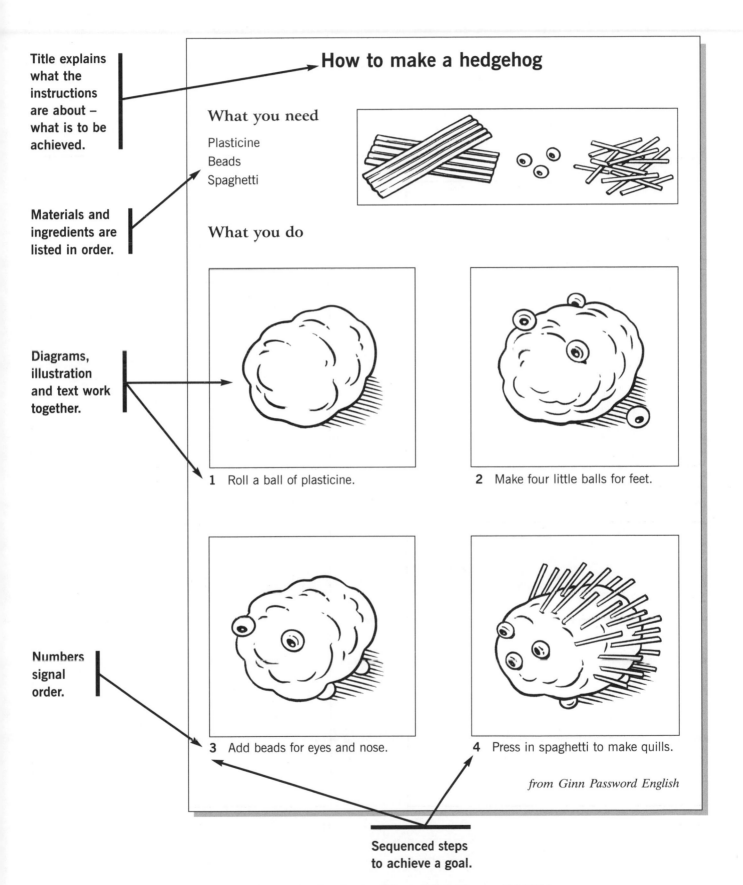

How to make a hedgehog

What you need

Plasticine
Beads
Spaghetti

What you do

1   Roll a ball of plasticine.

2   Make four little balls for feet.

3   Add beads for eyes and nose.

4   Press in spaghetti to make quills.

from Ginn Password English

Sequenced steps to achieve a goal.

Classworks Literacy Year 1 © Louise Gilbert, Nelson Thornes Ltd 2003

How to make a _____

What you need

What you do

1

2

3

4

(Pupil copymaster)

How to make a milkshake

Ingredients

A glass of milk

Four teaspoonfuls of cocoa

Two scoops of ice cream

Chocolate

Blender

First, put the milk in the blender.

Next, put in two scoops of ice cream

Next, add four teaspoonfuls of cocoa.

Next, turn on the blender.

Pour the milkshake into a glass.

Then, add the chocolate.

Drink!

from Make a Milkshake, *by Amanda McArthur Christie*

(Exemplar material)

Example of analysis of *How to make a milkshake*

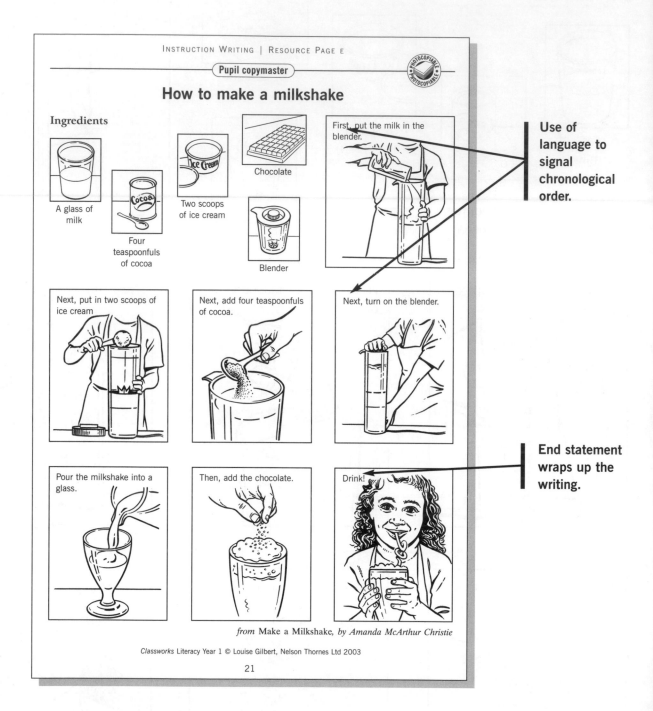

(Exemplar material)

Checklists for instruction writing

Checklist of general features of a set of instructions

- Title explains what instructions will help you do

- 'What you need' box is included with materials/ingredients listed in order

- Numbers are used to help you read the instructions in order

- Illustrations and text work together

- Instructions are written in sequenced steps

Example of a checklist for improving instruction writing

- Use language that signals chronological order ('first', 'next', 'then', 'finally' and so on)

- Tantalise the reader with a statement at the beginning ('Have you ever wondered ...')

- Use end statements to wrap up the writing

Example of a checklist for writing simple instructions

- Write in the imperative (like giving an order)

- Use chronological order (sequenced steps to achieve a goal)

- Use short clear sentences so reader does not become muddled

- Use describing words (adjectives/ adverbs) only when necessary

Classworks Literacy Year 1 © Louise Gilbert, Nelson Thornes Ltd 2003

Marking ladder

Name: _____

Pupil	Objective	Teacher
	My title explains what the instructions will help you do.	
	My 'What you need' box lists materials in order.	
	My instructions are written in clear, sequenced steps.	
	My instructions are written in the imperative (giving an order).	
	My instructions are written in short sentences.	
	I have used language to signal chronology ('first', 'then', 'next').	
	My beginning statement tantalises the reader.	
	My end statement wraps up my writing.	
	Could someone who knows nothing about this successfully use my instructions?	
	What could I do to improve my instructions next time?	

Traditional Stories

Outcome

Write a simple traditional story

Objectives

Sentence

1 to expect reading to make sense and check if it does not, and to read aloud using expression appropriate to the grammar of the text.

2 to use awareness of the grammar of a sentence to decipher new or unfamiliar words, e.g. predict text from the grammar, read on, leave a gap and reread.

4 to recognise full stops and capital letters when reading and understand how they affect the way a passage is read.

5 to continue to demarcate sentences in writing, ending a sentence with a full stop.

Text

1 to reinforce and apply their word-level skills through shared and guided reading.

2 to use phonological, contextual, grammatical and graphic knowledge to work out, predict and check the meanings of unfamiliar words and to make sense of what they read.

4 to retell stories, giving the main points in sequence and to notice differences between written and spoken forms in retelling, e.g. by comparing oral versions with the written text; to refer to relevant phrases and sentences.

5 to identify and record some key features of story language from a range of stories, and to practise reading and using them, e.g. in oral retelling.

7 to discuss reasons for, or causes of, incidents in stories.

10 to identify and compare basic story elements, e.g. beginnings and endings in different stories.

14 to represent outlines of story plots using, e.g. captions, pictures, arrows to record main incidents in order.

16 to use some of the elements of known stories to structure own writing.

Planning frame

● Understand the structure of traditional stories.
● Write in the style of traditional stories.

How you could plan this unit

Day 1	Day 2	Day 3	Day 4	Day 5
Talk for writing What is a traditional story? Define the term and collect examples	**Talk for writing** Retelling a traditional story. Compare the written and spoken versions	Reading/Writing	Reading/Writing	**Reading/Writing** Rewrite the middle of a well-known traditional story
		Structuring a Story	*Beginning a Story*	

Day 6	Day 7	Day 8	Day 9	Day 10
Reading/Writing	**Reading/Writing** Story plan for the children's own traditional story	Reading/Writing	**Reading/Writing** Writing the middle of their own traditional story	**Reading/Writing** Writing the end of their own traditional story. Evaluation of written outcome
Ending a Story		*Using Language*		

25

Structuring a Story

Objectives

We will learn how a traditional story is structured, and sequence the story of *Little Red Riding Hood* and write a story plan

You need: Resource Pages H and I; a copy of *Little Red Riding Hood*; copies of pictures made from the book illustrating the main events in the story (no more than five or six).

Whole class work

- Read the story of *Little Red Riding Hood*, preferably in a big book format. Encourage the children to listen carefully to the order in which the events take place.

- Hand out copies of illustrations from the shared text to selected children. Invite them to stand in front of the class and sequence the pictures/events chronologically.

- Discuss the sequence of events firstly in specific terms: 'As she was playing in the garden, Red Riding Hood was asked by her mother to visit her grandma on the other side of the wood.' Then discuss events using more general terms: 'The opening introduces the setting and the characters', thus identifying the general structure of a traditional story (see Resource Page H, checklist 1 for ideas).

- *Can you suggest some more traditional tales? Do they fit this general structure?*

- Explain that over the next few days they will be rewriting the story of *Little Red Riding Hood* and in order to ensure that their finished story is structured correctly, it is necessary to write a story plan.

- Using a simple story plan proforma of a beginning, middle and end, demonstrate how to plot the story using brief notes rather than full sentences (see Resource Page I, example 5). Explain that the middle of the story incorporates: build-up of events, complications, and resulting events (see Resource Page H, checklist 1).

Independent, pair or guided work

- Encourage the children to write a story plan for *Little Red Riding Hood* using captions, pictures and arrows to record the main incidents in order. The checklist can be used as a guide for structuring their story correctly.

Plenary

- Invite a child to share their story plan. With reference to the checklist, analyse the plan to ensure they have made reference to each structural element. *Does the plan detail the opening, event build-up, complication, resulting event, resolution and ending, in sequence?*

Beginning a Story

Objectives

We will identify the features of a traditional story beginning, and rewrite the beginning of *Little Red Riding Hood*

You need: Resource Pages A, B, H and I; whiteboards and markers (one between two).

Whole class work

- Read through the beginning of *Little Red Riding Hood* (Resource Page A).

- With response partners, the children discuss the type of information included and any features they notice. Allow time for the children to feed back their ideas. (See Resource Pages B and H for features to be identified and analysed.)

- *Why do you think this information is included? What effect do you think it has on the reader?*

- Analyse the features in turn, discussing their purpose and adding each to a class checklist. Encourage the children to brainstorm traditional story openings and ideas for creating setting (time, place, weather). Incorporate suggestions into the checklist.

- Demonstrate rewriting the beginning of *Little Red Riding Hood* using the features identified in checklist 2, Resource Page H. A model you could use is given in example 6, Resource Page I.

- When writing, take the opportunity to reinforce the use of phonic strategies.

- The children orally rehearse the first sentence for their own rewriting, then use a whiteboard to scribe their ideas, selecting a traditional opening and using capital letters and full stops appropriately. Share and explore the children's examples, asking them to explain their word choices.

Independent, pair or guided work

- Using the class checklist, the children rewrite the beginning of *Little Red Riding Hood*.

Plenary

- Ask several children to share their work. As a class, analyse their use of the features identified in the class checklist. *Does their beginning capture the reader's interest? Does their use of descriptive language create images for the reader?*

- Select one descriptive sentence to redraft. Encourage the children to brainstorm appropriate adverbs, adjectives or expressive verbs that would improve the sentence.

Ending a Story

Objectives

We will identify the features a traditional story ending should include and rewrite the ending of *Little Red Riding Hood*

You need: Resource Pages C–F and H; a range of traditional stories.

Whole class work

- Refer back to checklist 1 (Resource Page H), detailing the structure of a traditional story. Explain that today's lesson will examine what makes a good resolution and ending to a story.

- *Why do you think endings are so important? What would happen if you did not have a suitable ending?*

- Read through the endings from *The Three Little Pigs* (Resource Page C) and *Goldilocks and the Three Bears* (Resource Page E). With response partners, the children should identify the features that contribute to a good traditional story ending (see Resource Pages D and F for ideas).

- As they feed back ideas, encourage them to make links between the two texts: both texts possess a traditional story ending; both stories end happily for the 'good' character(s).

- Ensure all the points outlined are analysed and incorporated into a class checklist for successful story endings (see checklist 4, Resource Page H for ideas).

- Clarify the point that endings should not be rushed – the dilemma must be satisfactorily resolved.

- With response partners, the children recall the resolution and ending of *Little Red Riding Hood*. Using the class checklist and the children's contributions, together write an ending for the story incorporating all the relevant features. Challenge the children's contributions in order to refine their understanding and compositional skills.

Independent, pair or guided work

- Using the checklist created in whole class work, the children rewrite the ending of *Little Red Riding Hood*.

Plenary

- Ask the children to share their story ending with a partner. The partner should analyse their use of the features detailed in the class checklist and feed back two positive comments and one area for development.

- Share a range of other traditional story endings (for example *The Gingerbread Man*, *Cinderella*, *Jack and the Beanstalk*). Assess whether these endings also incorporate the features identified. Collect a range of traditional story endings (for example, 'From this day to that …') and add to the class checklist.

Using Language

Objectives

We will write a traditional story beginning, and use descriptive language to capture the reader's interest and describe a character

You need: Resource Pages G and H; whiteboards and pens.

Whole class work

- Explain that today the children will be writing the beginning of their traditional story.

- Using checklist 2 (Resource Page H), recall the features necessary for a good story beginning. Focus on the fact that many of the features require descriptive writing (describing time, place, weather, character, and so on). Inform the children that the focus of the shared session will be on developing their ability to write descriptively.

- Write the following sentence on the board:

> The cat went along the path.

- Ask the children to think of some words to describe the cat, the path and the way it moved and incorporate them into the sentence, for example:

> The stripy cat slunk along the narrow path.

- Reinforce the fact that descriptive language is used to engage a reader's interest.

- Write another sentence on the board:

> The boy went to the shop.

  Ask the children, in pairs, to improve the sentence by adding descriptive words. Share examples, prompting the children to discuss word choices.

- Remind the children that a good story beginning incorporates the introduction of the character(s). Read through *The Beast with a Thousand Teeth* (Resource Page G), encouraging the class to close their eyes as you read the description of the beast. Can the children visualise the character clearly? Reread and ask the children to underline the words that help to create a picture in the reader's mind.

- Ask the children to think of the main character they have chosen for their own traditional tale. Using a whiteboard, the children write a detailed description.

- Share descriptions. Discuss and list words that are powerful in creating an image.

Independent, pair or guided work

- Using the checklist created in whole class work the children write the beginning of their own traditional tale incorporating the use of descriptive language.

Plenary

- Share some of the children's story beginnings. Encourage the class to close their eyes when listening. *How effective is the writing in creating an image for the reader? Does it leave the reader wondering what will happen next?*

- Select one sentence and rewrite it with the words in a different order. Discuss what effect this has on the sentence. *Does it make the sentence more interesting?*

Pupil copymaster

Little Red Riding Hood – the opening

Once upon a time, on the edge of the big wood, there lived a little girl called Little Red Riding Hood. Her real name was Brenda but she was always known as Little Red Riding Hood because this is what her mother called her when she was a baby.

Brenda used to wear a red bonnet when she went out for a ride in her pram, and she still wears it now. One day, Little Red Riding Hood was playing out in the sunshine when her mother called her, "I want you to go over to Grandma's house with some groceries. Grandma's not very well and she hasn't been able to get out to the shops."

Jonathan Langley (HarperCollins)

(Exemplar analysis)

Example of analysis of *Little Red Riding Hood*

Use of a traditional story start.

Setting is established.

Character is introduced.

Descriptive language is used to capture the reader's interest.

Opening makes the reader wonder what will happen.

Once upon a time, on the edge of the big wood, there lived a little girl called Little Red Riding Hood. Her real name was Brenda but she was always known as Little Red Riding Hood because this is what her mother called her when she was a baby.

Brenda used to wear a red bonnet when she went out for a ride in her pram, and she still wears it now. One day, Little Red Riding Hood was playing out in the sunshine when her mother called her, "I want you to go over to Grandma's house with some groceries. Grandma's not very well and she hasn't been able to get out to the shops."

Jonathan Langley (HarperCollins)

Pupil copymaster

The Three Little Pigs – the ending

The little pig was very frightened, but he said nothing. He put a big pot of water on the fire to boil.

The wolf climbed on to the roof. Then he began to come down the chimney.

The pig took the lid from the pot. Into the pot fell the wolf, with a big splash. And that was the end of the wolf.

Ladybird Easy Read

(Exemplar analysis)

Example of analysis of *The Three Little Pigs – the ending*

The little pig was very frightened, but he said nothing. He put a big pot of water on the fire to boil.

The wolf climbed on to the roof. Then he began to come down the chimney.

The pig took the lid from the pot. Into the pot fell the wolf, with a big splash. And that was the end of the wolf.

Ladybird Easy Read

Dilemma resolved.

Happy ending (for the good character!).

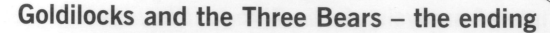

(Pupil copymaster)

Goldilocks and the Three Bears – the ending

At the sound of their voices, Goldilocks woke up. When she saw the three bears she was so frightened that she jumped out of bed, ran down the stairs, out of the house and into the wood as fast as she could. By the time the three bears reached the door, Goldilocks was gone. From that day on, the three bears never saw Goldilocks again, and they lived happily ever after.

Ladybird Books

(Exemplar analysis)

Example of analysis of *Goldilocks and the Three Bears*

Character realises they have been bad/wrong.

At the sound of their voices, Goldilocks woke up. When she saw the three bears she was so frightened that she jumped out of bed, ran down the stairs, out of the house and into the wood as fast as she could. By the time the three bears reached the door, Goldilocks was gone. From that day on, the three bears never saw Goldilocks again, and they lived happily ever after.

Ladybird Books

Traditional story ending.

(**Pupil copymaster**)

The Beast with a Thousand Teeth

A long time ago, in a land far away, the most terrible beast that ever lived roamed the countryside. It had four eyes, six legs and a thousand teeth. In the morning it would gobble up men as they went to work in the fields. In the afternoon it would break into lonely farms and eat up mothers and children as they sat down to lunch, and at night it would stalk the streets of towns, looking for its supper.

Terry Jones

Classworks Literacy Year 1 © Louise Gilbert, Nelson Thornes Ltd 2003

(Exemplar material)

Checklists for traditional stories

Example of a checklist for traditional story structure

- Opening includes setting and introduces the character
- A series of events build up
- Complications occur
- Events are described
- There is a resolution and ending

Example of a checklist for a traditional story beginning ②

- Use a traditional start:
  'Once upon a time'
  'One day'
  'A long time ago'
  'In a land far away'
  'There once was a'
- Create setting:
  Time – morning, night, noon, dusk
  Place – near the wood, on a hillside, in a valley, in a town
  Weather – stormy, sunny, cloudy, rainy
- Introduce the characters – contrasting good and bad
- Use descriptive language to capture the reader's interest
- Opening should leave the reader wondering what will happen

Example of a checklist for a traditional story middle

- Possibly use a repetitive structure ('Run, run as fast as you can', 'He huffed and he puffed' and so on)
- Make one event lead on to the next
- Use some short sentences to be dramatic
- Use suspense words:
  'Once upon a time'
  'Suddenly'
  'All of a sudden'
  'Without warning'
- Use descriptive language (adverbs, adjectives, expressive verbs, similes)

Example of a checklist for a traditional story ending

- The dilemma is resolved
- The character realises they have been wrong
- There is a happy ending
- Use a traditional story ending:
  'And they all lived happily ever after.'
  'And the next day they were married.'
  'And from that day to this she never ...'
  'And she/he never ...'

Continued ...

(Exemplar material)

Checklists for traditional stories

Example of a writing model for *Little Red Riding Hood* ⑤

- Beginning
  Red Riding Hood told to go to Grandma's, Grandma is sick, lives on other side of wood

- Middle
  Red Riding Hood meets wolf in wood, wolf goes to Grandma's, wolf eats Grandma and gets into her bed, Red Riding Hood arrives, wolf tries to eat Red Riding Hood

- End
  Woodcutter arrives, wolf is killed, Grandma is rescued

Example of a first paragraph for *Little Red Riding Hood* ⑥

There once was a young girl called Little Red Riding Hood who lived with her mother and father on the edge of a large wood. Her curly blonde hair shimmered gold and her eyes were a sparkling blue. One bright and sunny morning, as the birds were singing, Little Red Riding Hood carefully placed some groceries into a wicker basket and skipped off down the path towards her sick grandmother's house.

(Marking ladder)

Name: _____

Pupil	Objective	Teacher
	I have used a traditional story start.	
	My beginning creates a setting.	
	My beginning introduces the characters.	
	In the middle of my story one event leads to the next.	
	I have used descriptive language.	
	My story ending resolves the problem.	
	I have used a traditional story ending.	
	What could I do to improve my story next time?	

Simple Dictionaries

Outcome

A simple dictionary for the Reception Class

Objectives	
	Sentence
	5 to continue demarcating sentences in writing, ending a sentence with a full stop.
	Text
	20 to use simple dictionaries, and to understand their alphabetical organisation.
	25 to assemble information from own experience; to use simple sentences to describe, based on examples from reading.

Planning frame	
	● Understand alphabetical order.
	● Use dictionaries for spelling and definitions of words.

How you could plan this unit

Day 1	Day 2	Day 3	Day 4	Day 5
Talk for writing	Reading	Writing Organising words into alphabetical order – (exploring what happens when two words begin with the same letter)	Reading/Writing	Reading/Writing
Alphabetical Order	*Using a Dictionary*		*Making a Dictionary*	*Writing Definitions*

Alphabetical Order

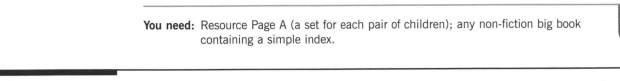

Objective

We will understand whut is meant by èalphabetical orderê

You need: Resource Page A (a set for each pair of children); any non-fiction big book containing a simple index.

Whole class work

● Ask the children if they know what is meant by the term 'alphabet'. Discuss the children's ideas.

> The alphabet is a list of all the letters we use in writing. We organise the letters of the alphabet into an order, which we call èalphabetical orderê.

● Encourage the children to sing through an alphabet song or chant it several times to establish the correct order, then challenge different groups to remember the correct sequence.

● Using Resource Page A, give one letter card each to 26 children. Ask any remaining children to help organise the others into alphabetical order.

● Explain that alphabetical order is used as a way of organising information. Recall making an index for an information book and show an example of an index in any non-fiction shared text. Ensure the children understand how the information is organised.

Independent, pair or guided work

● Provide each pair of the children with a set of alphabet cards. Ask each pair to organise the letters into alphabetical order. Encourage the children to share strategies for recalling the correct order.

● Once the letters have been placed in alphabetical order, one member of the pair hides their eyes, while their partner turns over a card. The partner then challenges the other to identify the missing letter, using the letter before and the letter after as a clue.

Plenary

● Play a 'guess the letter' game to extend the children's understanding of alphabetical order. Explain that you have selected a letter and give clues which will assist them in identifying it, for example, *I'm thinking of a letter near the beginning of the alphabet which comes after 'b' and before 'e'.*

● Discuss what would make a sensible guess. What more information would be needed to be sure the letter is correctly identified?

● Less able children could be given a copy of the alphabet to assist them. More able children could call out the questions, once confident.

Using a Dictionary

Objectives

We will learn what a dictionary is used for, and use a dictionary to locate information

You need: Resource Pages A and B; simple dictionaries (one between two), a variety of small objects starting with different letters (e.g. car, pen).

Whole class work

- Ask the children: *Do you know what a 'hive' is? What type of book could you use to find out what the word means?* If nobody suggests using a dictionary, show the children a simple example and explain that a dictionary can be used to find out the meaning of a word and to check on how it is spelt.

- Flick through the pages of the dictionary. *What do you notice about the way the information is organised?* Explain that in a dictionary the words are organised alphabetically.

- Explain that the children are going to make themselves into a dictionary to help them understand how one can be used to locate information. Hand out the alphabet cards (Resource Page A) as before and ask these 26 children to organise themselves into alphabetical order. Reinforce the fact that this is how a dictionary is organised, with all words beginning with 'a' at the beginning and all the words beginning with 'z' at the end.

- Hand an object, for example, a toy car, to a child without a letter. Explain that if you wanted to find the word 'car' in the dictionary you would need to identify its first letter. Ask the child holding the object to confirm the first letter and then find the child holding the corresponding letter. Repeat with a variety of objects with differing initial letters.

- Ask a child to locate the word 'hive' in a dictionary and read out the definition using the knowledge they have just acquired.

Independent, pair or guided work

- Give the children word cards (Resource Page B) and ask them to locate the words in a simple dictionary. Higher attaining children could note the meaning of the word whereas lower attaining members of the group could simply note other words entered under the same letter.

Plenary

- Read out a word from the dictionary. Ask the children to name other words that begin with the same letter. Ask the children to think about how all the words beginning with the same letter could be organised.

Making a Dictionary

Objectives

We will enter words into a dictionary, and develop our understanding of alphabetical order

You need: Resource Pages A, C, D and G–K.

Whole class work

- The children sit in a circle. Hand out the alphabet cards (Resource Page A), one per child, in alphabetical order. Starting with the child holding 'a', begin to play 'I went to the market and bought ...', asking the child to think of an item beginning with that letter, for example:

> I went to the market and bought an apricot.

- Continue around the circle allowing each child to add something beginning with their letter ('I went to the market and bought an <u>a</u>pple, a <u>b</u>anana, a <u>c</u>arrot and a <u>d</u>ragon').

- For the children who don't have a letter, start again from 'a'.

- Explain that today they will be entering words into an empty or 'skeleton' dictionary by working through the alphabet and 'collecting' words that begin with each letter, just as they have done in the games they have played.

- Show the children a page from a simple dictionary (Resource Page C). Ask the children to discuss with response partners what they notice about the way the information is presented. Allow the children time to feed back ideas and discuss the points outlined in the exemplar analysis (Resource Page D). Assemble the ideas into a class checklist for writing a dictionary (see Resource Page K for ideas).

- Show the children the skeleton dictionary, *My First Dictionary* (Resource Pages G–J). Draw attention to some of the features and demonstrate how to enter a word into the dictionary (adding a picture to assist in the location of information). Outline strategies for attempting to write unknown words (for example, analogy, counting phonemes).

Independent, pair or guided work

- Give each child a skeleton dictionary into which they enter one word and an accompanying picture for each letter of the alphabet. Lower attaining children could produce a 'group' dictionary by completing a given number of letters each.

Plenary

- In mixed ability pairs, the children can take it in turns to show their partner their dictionary. Referring back to the class checklist created during the shared session, partners should provide feedback as to whether each word is entered clearly and whether the illustrations assist the reader in accessing the information quickly and easily.

Writing Definitions

Objective

We will write a definition for a word

You need: Resource Pages E, F, K and L; Post-it™ notes; whiteboards and pens (one between two); classroom objects – pencil, paintbrush, book and so on.

Whole class work

- Remind the children of the work they began in the previous lesson. Recall that dictionaries can be used to locate a word (perhaps to assist spelling), and can also be used to find out what a word means.

- Explain that today they will explore more features that dictionaries use to assist readers, and learn how to write a definition for a word.

- Look at the page of words that begin with 'b' (Resource Pages E and F). *What other features can you see? Why is one of the letters in the margin highlighted? How do you think this would help a reader?*

- *A definition tells the reader what a word means.* Put Post-it™ notes over the definitions on the page and uncover one. Read it together. Ask the children to discuss anything they notice about the way it is written. Draw out:
  - use of a full sentence
  - explanation is clear and concise to give the reader the information they require quickly and to avoid confusion.

- Uncover the other definitions. *Do the features identified in the first example apply?* Note the repeated use of 'A _____ is ...'.

- Add the additional features identified to the class checklist started during the previous lesson (see Resource Page K for ideas).

Independent, pair or guided work

- Hold up a classroom object, for example, a pencil. Ask the children to work with a partner to think of a definition beginning with 'A pencil is ...'. Once the children have orally rehearsed their sentence they can scribe it on to a whiteboard. Ask the children to hold up their whiteboards. Check the work for use of a capital letter and a full stop.

- Using the skeleton dictionaries begun in the previous lesson, the children add definitions to the words they entered.

Plenary

- Read a definition from one of the children's dictionaries and ask the rest of the class to guess the word it relates to.

- Select three children of differing abilities to share their finished dictionaries. Working through the marking ladder (Resource Page L), ask the class to 'assess' the three pieces. Recall how each feature is important in assisting the reader.

- The dictionaries may now be gathered together and given to the Reception Class to use as a resource.

Pupil copymaster

Alphabet cards

a	b	c	d	e
f	g	h	i	j
k	l	m	n	o
p	q	r	s	t
u	v	w	x	y
z				

Word cards

van	key
jam	ice
sock	x-ray
dinosaur	ball
dog	arm
plant	school
zoo	gate
bicycle	envelope
mountain	television

Pupil copymaster

Words beginning with 'd'

dinosaur

D d

duck

dog

digger

(Exemplar analysis)

Example of analysis of *Words beginning with 'd'*

Capital and
lower case
letters are given.

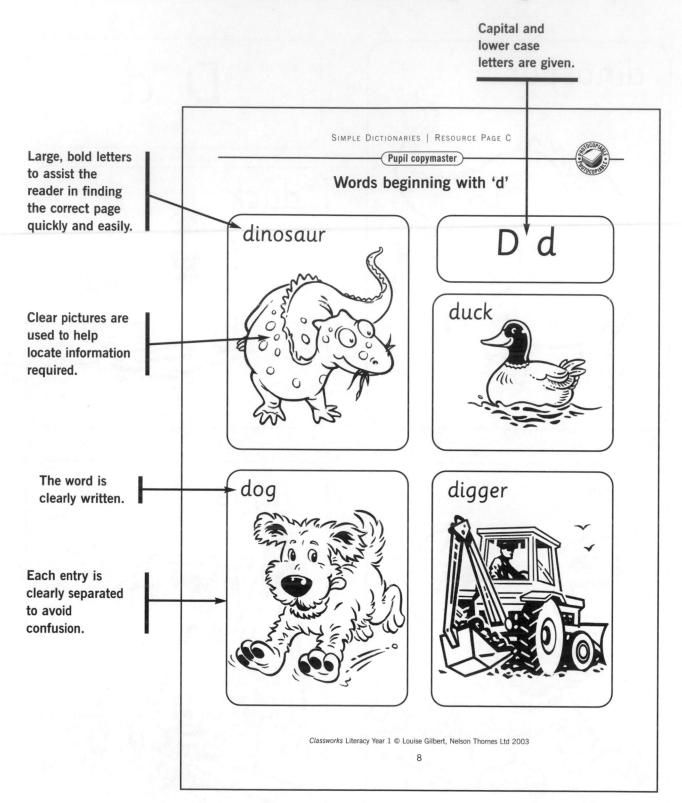

(Pupil copymaster)

Words beginning with 'd'

Large, bold letters to assist the reader in finding the correct page quickly and easily.

dinosaur

D d

Clear pictures are used to help locate information required.

duck

The word is clearly written.

dog

digger

Each entry is clearly separated to avoid confusion.

Classworks Literacy Year 1 © Louise Gilbert, Nelson Thornes Ltd 2003

8

Classworks Literacy Year 1 © Louise Gilbert, Nelson Thornes Ltd 2003

Pupil copymaster

Words beginning with 'b'

a **b** c d e f g h i j k l m n o p q r s t u v w x y z

Bb

bed – You sleep in a bed.

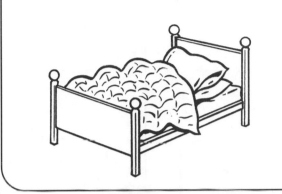

ball – A ball is round. You can play games with it.

bear – A bear is a big furry animal.

banana – A banana is a long yellow fruit.

bicycle – A bicycle has two wheels. You ride a bicycle.

(Exemplar analysis)

Example of analysis of *Words beginning with 'b'*

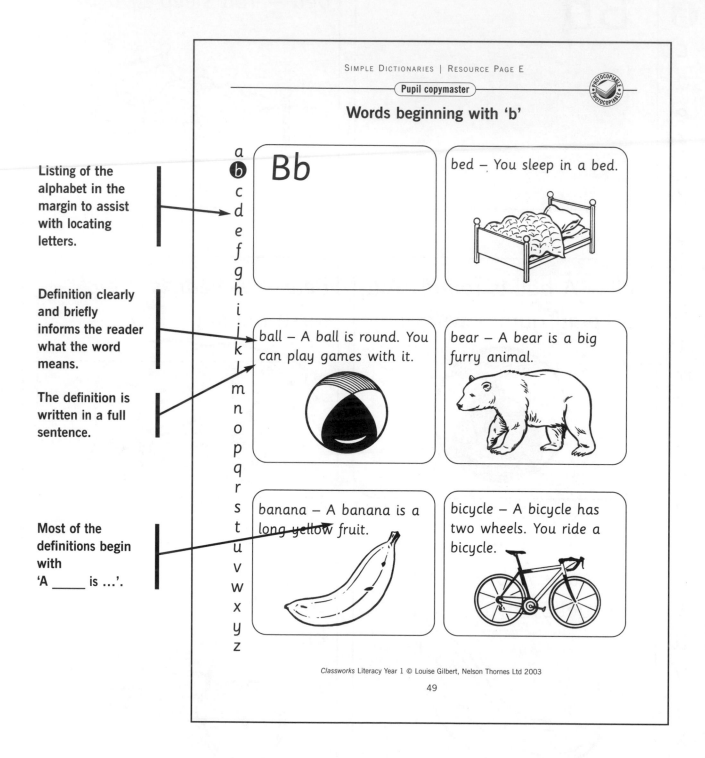

Listing of the alphabet in the margin to assist with locating letters.

Definition clearly and briefly informs the reader what the word means.

The definition is written in a full sentence.

Most of the definitions begin with 'A _____ is ...'.

Within the pupil copymaster:

SIMPLE DICTIONARIES | RESOURCE PAGE E

(Pupil copymaster)

Words beginning with 'b'

a
b
c
d
e
f
g
h
i
j
k
l
m
n
o
p
q
r
s
t
u
v
w
x
y
z

Bb

bed – You sleep in a bed.

ball – A ball is round. You can play games with it.

bear – A bear is a big furry animal.

banana – A banana is a long yellow fruit.

bicycle – A bicycle has two wheels. You ride a bicycle.

Classworks Literacy Year 1 © Louise Gilbert, Nelson Thornes Ltd 2003

49

Pupil copymaster

My First Dictionary

A

is for Apple

Name: _____

7

Yy

Zz

a b c d e f g h i j k l m n o p q r s t u v w x y z

Pupil copymaster

a b c d e f g h i j k l m n o p q r s t u v w x y z

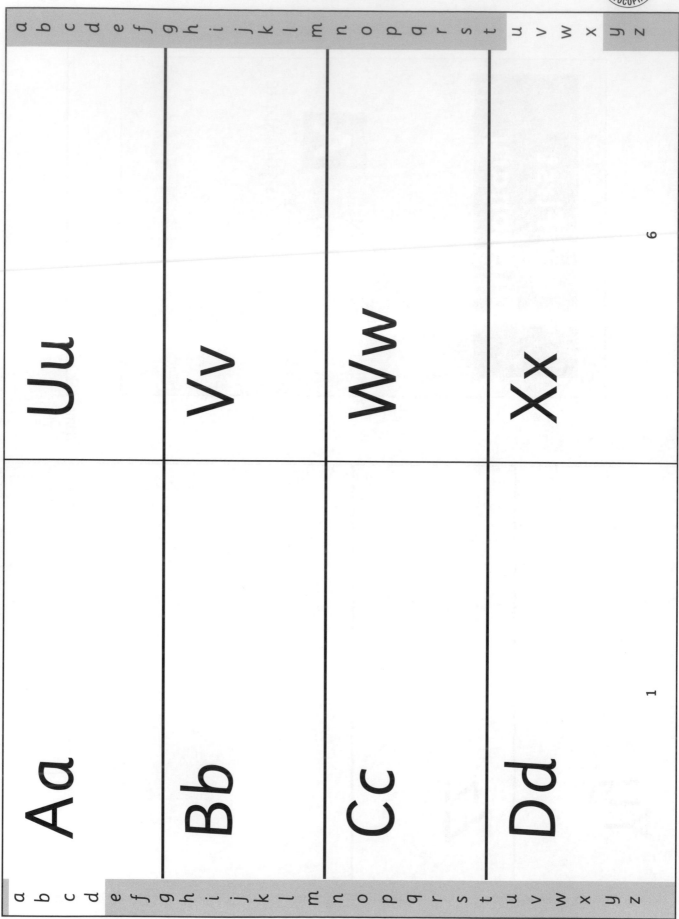

Uu

Vv

Ww

Xx

6

Aa

Bb

Cc

Dd

1

a b c d e f g h i j k l m n o p q r s t u v w x y z

Pupil copymaster

a b c d	e f g h	i j k l m n o p q r s t	u v w x y z

Ee

Ff

Gg

Hh

2

Qq

Rr

Ss

Tt

5

a b c d e f g h	i j k l m n o p	q r s t	u v w x y z

Classworks Literacy Year 1 © Louise Gilbert, Nelson Thornes Ltd 2003

Pupil copymaster

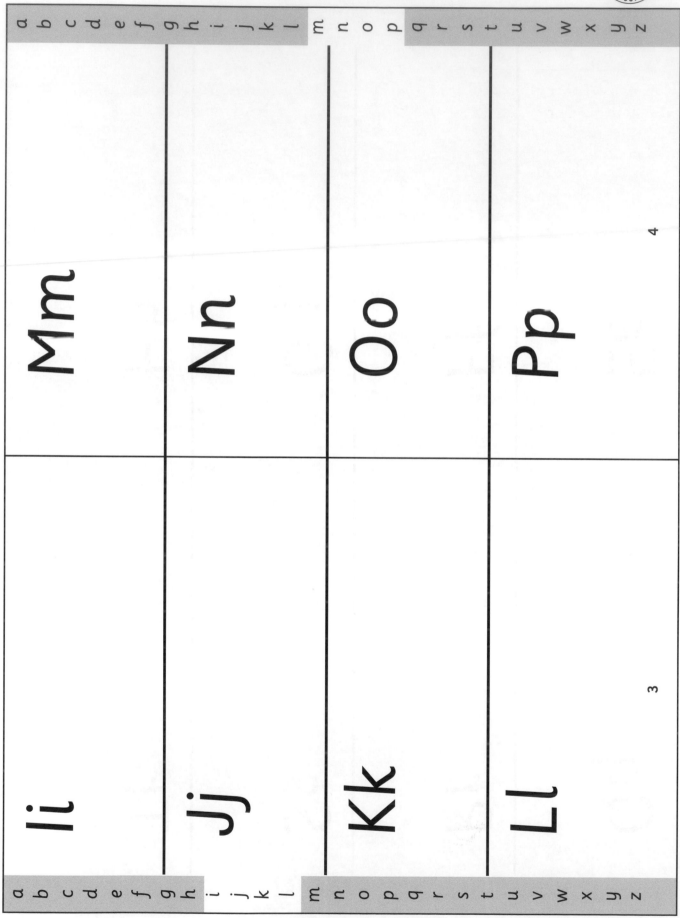

a b c d e f g h i j k l m n o p q r s t u v w x y z

Mm

Nn

Oo

Pp

Ii

Jj

Kk

Ll

4

3

a b c d e f g h i j k l m n o p q r s t u v w x y z

(Exemplar material)

Checklists for simple dictionaries

Example of a checklist for creating a very simple dictionary

- Write the letter of the alphabet in large bold type at the top of the page and give both the lower case and the capital letter

- Clearly separate entries

- Clearly illustrate each entry to help the reader locate information

- Make sure all words entered into the dictionary are clearly written

Example of a checklist for extending a simple dictionary

- List the alphabet in the margin and highlight relevant letter(s)

- Use page numbers

- Write definitions in full sentences

- Make definitions clear and concise

- A definition may begin with 'A _____ is …'

Classworks Literacy Year 1 © Louise Gilbert, Nelson Thornes Ltd 2003

(Marking ladder)

Name: _____

Pupil	Objective	Teacher
	I have written each word in my dictionary clearly.	
	I have illustrated each dictionary entry clearly to help the reader locate information.	
	I have written my definitions in full sentences.	
	My definitions are clear and concise.	
	What could I do to improve my dictionary next time?	

Stories With a Pattern

Outcome

A story with a predictable, repetitive pattern rewritten by substituting key words

Objectives

Sentence

1 to expect written text to make sense and to check for sense if it does not.

3 to draw on grammatical awareness, to read with appropriate expression and intonation, e.g. in reading to others, or to dolls, puppets.

4 to write captions and simple sentences, and to reread, recognising whether or not they make sense, e.g. missing words, wrong word order.

8 to begin using full stops to demarcate sentences.

9 to use a capital letter for the personal pronoun 'I' and for the start of a sentence.

Text

2 to use phonological, contextual, grammatical and graphic knowledge to work out, predict and check the meanings of unfamiliar words and to make sense of what they read.

3 to notice the difference between spoken and written forms through retelling known stories; compare oral versions with the written text.

7 to re-enact stories in a variety of ways, e.g. through role-play, using dolls or puppets.

8 through shared and guided writing to apply phonological, graphic knowledge and sight vocabulary to spell words accurately.

11 to make simple picture storybooks with sentences, modelling them on basic text conventions, e.g.: cover, author's name, title, layout.

Planning frame

- Identify and recognise repetitive patterns.

- Use predictable structures to substitute words to create an individual piece of work.

How you could plan this unit

Day 1	Day 2	Day 3	Day 4	Day 5
Talk for writing Collecting and sharing stories with predictable and repetitive patterns	Reading	Writing	Reading/Writing	Reading/Writing
	Dear Zoo	*A Different Zoo*	*We're Going on a Bear Hunt*	*Breaking the Pattern*

Dear Zoo

Objectives

We will learn why authors use repetitive or predictable patterns, and identify repetitive patterns within a text

You need: Resource Pages A and B (or a big book version of *Dear Zoo*, by Rod Campbell); plastic animals or pictures of the animals from the text (elephant, giraffe, lion, camel, snake, monkey, frog, puppy); red and green OHT pens.

Whole class work	• Read *Dear Zoo* (Resource Page A). If you have the big book version, select children to lift each flap. Discuss the children's immediate responses. ***Did you enjoy listening to the story? Which was your favourite part? Why? Which animal would you like to have as a pet?***
	• Reread the text, encouraging the children to join in. Ask your class to consider why they found it easy to join in with the retelling. Steer the children towards the author's use of a repetitive pattern. (See Resource Page B.)
	• Explain that authors use repetitive or predictable patterns to make their stories more fun and more memorable.
	• Using pictures or plastic animals, invite the children to sequence the animals as they appear in the book. Select individuals to retell the story using the animals as a prompt in combination with their knowledge of the repetitive pattern. Question the children throughout the retelling to develop understanding, for example, ***What will the next line be? How do you know?***
	• Show the children an enlarged copy of *Dear Zoo*. Read to the end of the third stanza and model how to locate the words/lines that form the repetitive pattern. Underline these in red. Underline the words that change in green.
Independent, pair or guided work	• Ask the children to identify the repetitive pattern by underlining in red the words or lines that are repeated.
	• Words that change through the text (and are not repeated) can be underlined in green.
Plenary	• Reread the last stanza asking a child to highlight the words that follow the repetitive pattern and those that do not – again using different coloured pens.
	• Look closely at the words that have been added or altered, 'thought very hard' and 'I kept him'. Explain that the author altered the pattern in order to draw the story to a close.

A Different Zoo

Objective

We will replace words in a story with a repetitive pattern

You need: Resource Pages A, C and D; plastic animals or pictures of the animals from the text (elephant, giraffe, lion, camel, snake, monkey, frog, puppy) plus an additional animal (for example, a crocodile); whiteboards and pens.

Whole class work

- Reread *Dear Zoo* (Resource Page A) then explain, **Today you are going to make your own version of Dear Zoo, replacing some words with your own ideas.**

- Using a piece of the children's work from the previous lesson, recall which words form the repetitive pattern and therefore can't be altered (highlighted red), and which can be substituted without affecting the pattern (highlighted green).

- Prompt the children to look closely at the words highlighted green in stanzas 2–7. In pairs, the children consider what type of words they are and how they are linked: the first word is an animal's name and the second word describes that animal.

- Using the plastic animals and the sheet of useful words (Resource Page D), invite the children to match each word to the corresponding creature. Discuss why each word is suited to that particular animal.

- Hold up a plastic animal not used in the text (for example, a crocodile). Ask the children, in pairs, to think of a word that describes the creature and to give a reason why it may not be suitable as a pet. Encourage each pair to scribe their ideas on to a whiteboard. Share some examples asking the children to discuss their choice of word. **Which words are more suitable than others? Why?**

- Show the children a copy of the *Dear Zoo* letter (Resource Page C), which is a writing frame to assist them in creating their own version of *Dear Zoo*. Ensure the children understand that the first three stanzas must incorporate unsuitable animals while the fourth should be a 'perfect pet'.

Independent, pair or guided work

- Using the writing frame, the children enter alternative animals and appropriate describing words to create their own adaptation of *Dear Zoo*.

Plenary

- Selected children share their alternative *Dear Zoo*. Discuss whether they have made suitable substitutions to the original text. **How well do their describing words link to their chosen animals?**

We're Going on a Bear Hunt

Objectives

We will identify repetitive patterns within a more complex text, and learn to replace words within a repetitive text

You need: Resource Pages E, F and I; red and green marker pens; a blank zigzag book for each child (made from A3 paper cut in half horizontally and folded back and forth into thirds).

Whole class work

- Read *We're Going on a Bear Hunt* (Resource Page E).

- With assistance from the children, write the physical descriptions found in the text on to separate sheets of paper (for example, 'long wavy grass'). You may like to add simple pictures to assist lower attaining members of the group. As a class, work through the features sequencing them as they appear in the book.

- Using the sequenced features as a visual prompt and the repetitive pattern, begin to retell the story. Some children could mime the hunters going through the grass/mud/forest, and so on, and others could join in with the retelling.

- Once the children are confident at using the repetitive pattern orally, display an enlarged copy of *We're Going on a Bear Hunt*. Together, identify the repetitive pattern, underlining those words that do not change in red, and the interchangeable words in green. (See also Resource Page F.)

- Examine the words underlined in green. Discuss what type of words they are and how they relate to one another.
  - The physical feature is named – 'grass'.
  - The next line gives a more detailed description of the feature – 'long wavy grass'.
  - Then two words are put together to represent the sound made – 'swishy swashy'.
  - This is repeated three times.

- *You are going to write your own version of* **We're Going on a Bear Hunt**, *using a different animal and different words to describe it.*

- As a class choose an animal and a physical feature not mentioned in the book (for example, a lion and a thunderstorm) and model how to write an additional verse (see example 2, Resource Page I).

- Together, create a class checklist for writing a predictable, repetitive story (see Resource Page I for ideas).

Independent, pair or guided work

- The children write the title on the cover of their blank zigzag book.

- Using the repetitive pattern identified during the shared session, the children write three verses to begin their hunt.

Plenary

- Invite some children to share their work. As a class, assess their use of the repetitive pattern and their choice of substituted words. *Do the words relate well to one another?*

Breaking the Pattern

We will rewrite a poem with a break in the repetitive pattern

You need: Resource Pages G–J; zigzag books from previous lesson.

Whole class work

- Read the Tiptoe section of *We're Going on a Bear Hunt*, where the hunters find the bear (Resource Page G).

- *What do you notice about the repetitive pattern? Why do you think the author stopped using it?*

- Explain that a break in a repetitive pattern creates dramatic effect, in this case, building suspense.

- Analyse how the writer has created the suspense by gradually building up a picture of the creature (see Resource Page H). Ask the children to discuss the use of capitals.

- Thinking about the animal they selected in the previous lesson, the children decide which words they could include in their own rewriting of the story and which they may have to substitute.

- Select one child's choice of animal, for example, a lion. Identify which words from the original text need to be substituted and model an alternative version (see example 3, Resource Page I).

- Refer back to the pictures that accompany the Tiptoe section of text. Ensure that the children understand the importance of incorporating all the features of the animal they describe (for example, the big shaggy mane, huge yellow eyes) into the accompanying illustration.

Independent, pair or guided work

- Using a copy of the Tiptoe section, the children rewrite it, substituting words as necessary to describe their chosen animal.

- The children illustrate the cover of their books.

Plenary

- Using a copy of the marking ladder (Resource Page J), select one child's completed book and assess their work against it. Encourage the children to discuss any changes they would make to their work, given the opportunity to improve it.

(Pupil copymaster)

Dear Zoo

I wrote to the zoo to send me a pet.
They sent me an elephant.
He was too big!
I sent him back.

— ◆ —

So they sent me a giraffe.
He was too tall!
I sent him back.

— ◆ —

So they sent me a lion.
He was too fierce!
I sent him back.

— ◆ —

So they sent me a camel.
He was too grumpy!
I sent him back.

— ◆ —

So they sent me a snake.
He was too scary!
I sent him back.

— ◆ —

So they sent me a monkey.
He was too naughty!
I sent him back.

— ◆ —

So they sent me a frog.
He was too jumpy!
I sent him back.

— ◆ —

So they thought very hard, and sent me a puppy.
He was perfect!
I kept him.

Rod Campbell (Puffin Books)

(**Exemplar analysis**)

Example of analysis of *Dear Zoo*

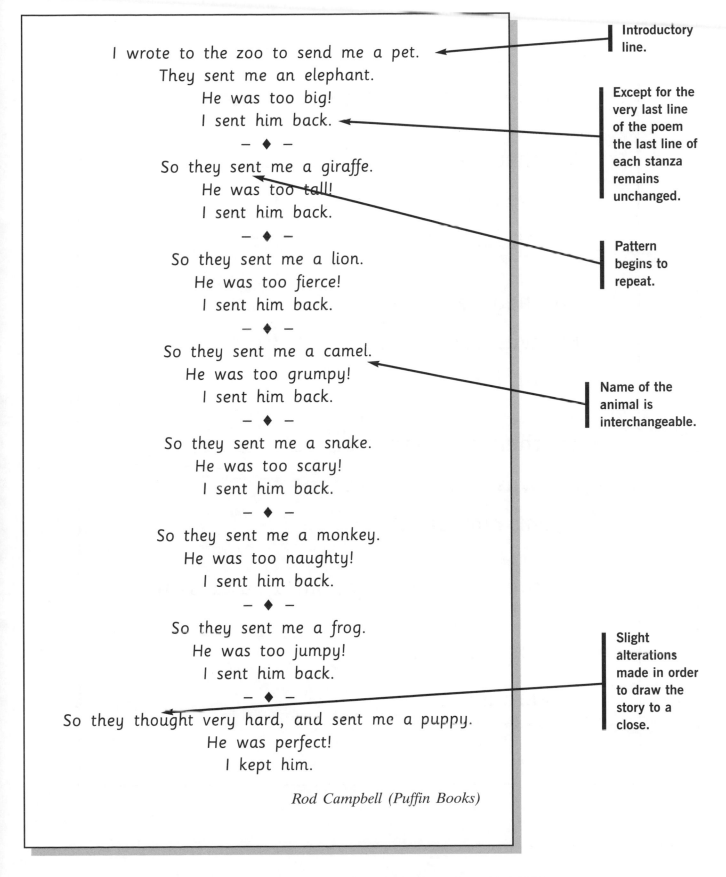

I wrote to the zoo to send me a pet. ← **Introductory line.**
They sent me an elephant.
He was too big!
I sent him back. ← **Except for the very last line of the poem the last line of each stanza remains unchanged.**

– ◆ –

So they sent me a giraffe. ← **Pattern begins to repeat.**
He was too tall!
I sent him back.

– ◆ –

So they sent me a lion.
He was too fierce!
I sent him back.

– ◆ –

So they sent me a camel.
He was too grumpy! ← **Name of the animal is interchangeable.**
I sent him back.

– ◆ –

So they sent me a snake.
He was too scary!
I sent him back.

– ◆ –

So they sent me a monkey.
He was too naughty!
I sent him back.

– ◆ –

So they sent me a frog.
He was too jumpy!
I sent him back.

– ◆ –

So they thought very hard, and sent me a puppy. ← **Slight alterations made in order to draw the story to a close.**
He was perfect!
I kept him.

Rod Campbell (Puffin Books)

(Pupil copymaster)

Dear Zoo letter

I wrote to the zoo to send me a pet.

So they sent me a _____.

He was too _____!

I sent him back.

So they sent me a _____.

He was too _____!

I sent him back.

So they sent me a _____.

He was too _____!

I sent him back.

So they thought very hard, and sent me a _____.

He was perfect!

I kept him.

Pupil copymaster

Useful words

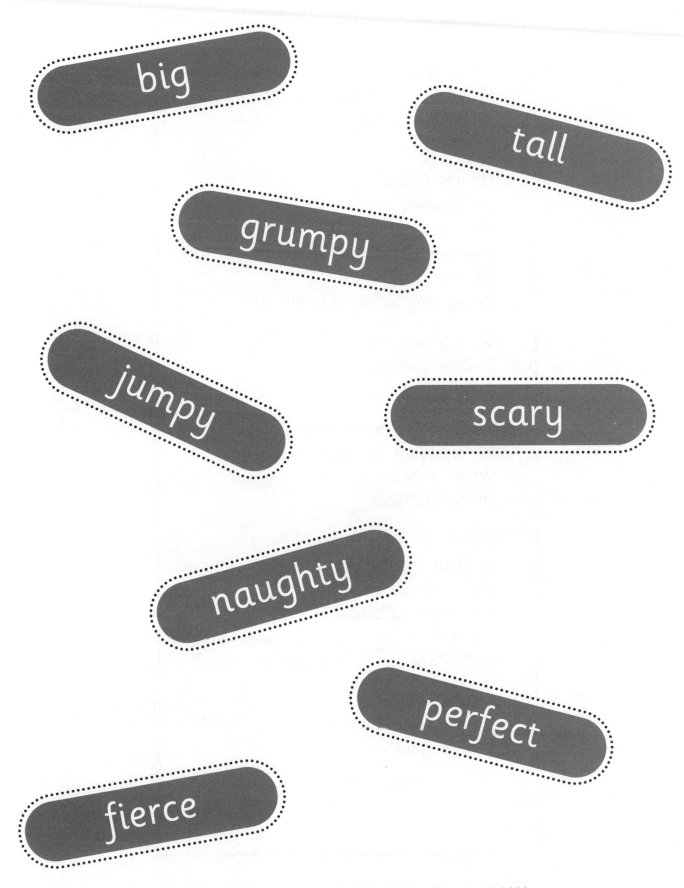

big

tall

grumpy

jumpy

scary

naughty

perfect

fierce

(**Pupil copymaster**)

We're Going on a Bear Hunt

We're going on a bear hunt.
We're going to catch a big one.
What a beautiful day!
We're not scared.

Uh-uh! Grass!
Long wavy grass.
We can't go over it.
We can't go under it.
Oh no!
We've got to go through it!

Swishy swashy!
Swishy swashy!
Swishy swashy!

We're going on a bear hunt.
We're going to catch a big one.
What a beautiful day!
We're not scared.

Uh-uh! A river!
A deep cold river.
We can't go over it.
We can't go under it.
Oh no!
We've got to go through it!

Splash splosh!
Splash splosh!
Splash splosh!

from We're Going on a Bear Hunt,
by Michael Rosen

(Exemplar analysis)

Example of analysis of *We're Going on a Bear Hunt*

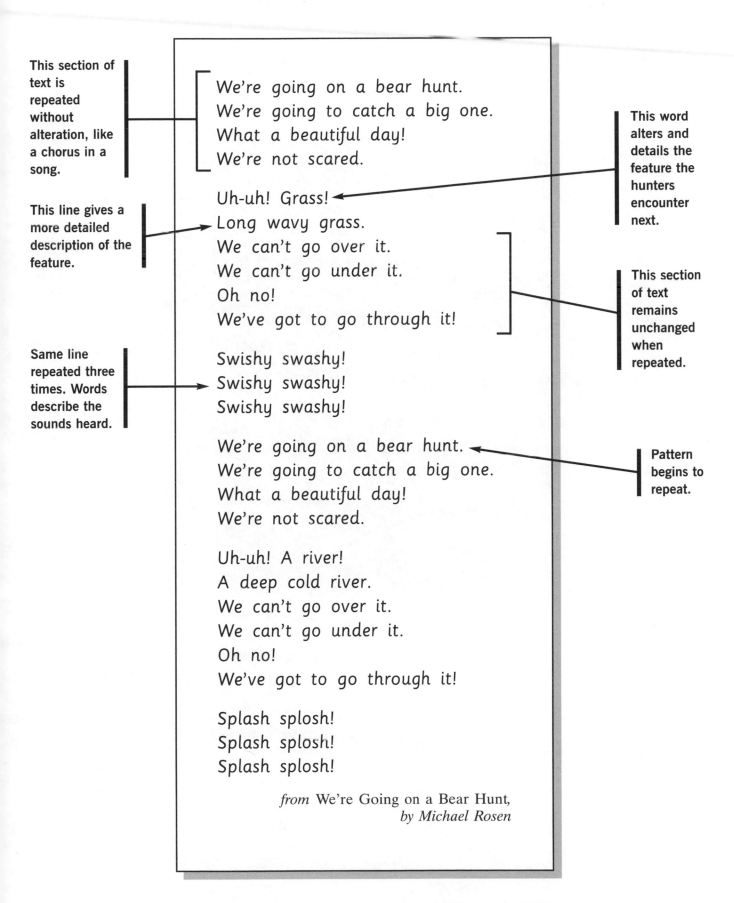

This section of text is repeated without alteration, like a chorus in a song.

We're going on a bear hunt.
We're going to catch a big one.
What a beautiful day!
We're not scared.

This word alters and details the feature the hunters encounter next.

This line gives a more detailed description of the feature.

Uh-uh! Grass!
Long wavy grass.
We can't go over it.
We can't go under it.
Oh no!
We've got to go through it!

This section of text remains unchanged when repeated.

Same line repeated three times. Words describe the sounds heard.

Swishy swashy!
Swishy swashy!
Swishy swashy!

We're going on a bear hunt.
We're going to catch a big one.
What a beautiful day!
We're not scared.

Pattern begins to repeat.

Uh-uh! A river!
A deep cold river.
We can't go over it.
We can't go under it.
Oh no!
We've got to go through it!

Splash splosh!
Splash splosh!
Splash splosh!

from We're Going on a Bear Hunt,
by Michael Rosen

(Pupil copymaster)

We're Going on a Bear Hunt – Tiptoe section

Tiptoe!

Tiptoe!

Tiptoe!

WHAT'S THAT?

One shiny wet nose!
Two big furry ears!
Two big goggly eyes!

IT'S A BEAR!!!!

from We're Going on a Bear Hunt,
by Michael Rosen

(Exemplar analysis)

Example of analysis of Tiptoe section

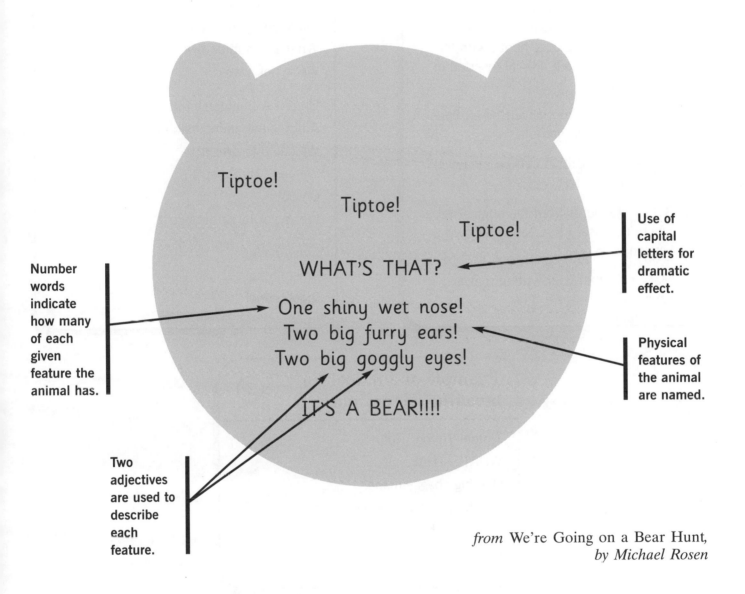

Tiptoe!

Tiptoe!

Tiptoe!

WHAT'S THAT?

One shiny wet nose!
Two big furry ears!
Two big goggly eyes!

IT'S A BEAR!!!!

Use of capital letters for dramatic effect.

Number words indicate how many of each given feature the animal has.

Physical features of the animal are named.

Two adjectives are used to describe each feature.

from We're Going on a Bear Hunt,
by Michael Rosen

(Exemplar material)

Checklist and models for stories with a pattern

Example of a checklist for rewriting a patterned story ①

- Include on the front cover a title modelled on the original text, 'We're going on a _____ hunt', with the name of a different animal inserted in the space

- Include on the front cover the author's name (your own name)

- Follow the repetitive pattern modelled in the original text

- Substitute words from the original text where necessary to create your own version

- Make sure that your writing makes sense

Example of a model for a story with a pattern ②

We're going on a lion hunt
We're going to catch a big one
What a beautiful day!
We're not scared

Uh-uh! A thunderstorm!
A big, black thunderstorm
We can't go over it
We can't go under it
Oh no!
We've got to go through it!

Crash bang!
Crash bang!
Crash bang!

Example of a model for breaking a story pattern ③

Tiptoe! Tiptoe! Tiptoe!
WHAT'S THAT?
One big shaggy mane!
Two huge yellow eyes!
Four large heavy paws!
IT'S A LION!!!!

Marking ladder

Name: _____

Pupil	Objective	Teacher
	My front cover includes a title 'We're going on a _____ hunt'.	
	My front cover includes the author's name (my own name).	
	My story follows the repetitive pattern modelled in the original text.	
	I have substituted words from the original text where necessary to create a new version.	
	My pictures relate well to the text.	
	My writing makes sense!	
	What could I do to improve my story next time?	

Stories of Fantasy Worlds

Outcome

A simple fantasy story

Objectives

Sentence

1 to expect reading to make sense and check if it does not.

2 to use awareness of the grammar of a sentence to decipher new or unfamiliar words, e.g. predict text from the grammar, read on, leave a gap and reread.

4 [be taught] about word order, e.g. by reordering sentences, predicting words from previous text, grouping a range of words that might 'fit', and discussing the reasons why.

5 other common uses of capitalisation, e.g. for personal titles ('Mr', 'Miss'), headings, book titles, emphasis.

Text

1 to reinforce and apply their word-level skills through shared and guided reading.

2 to use phonological, contextual, grammatical and graphic knowledge to work out, predict and check the meanings of unfamiliar words and to make sense of what they read.

3 to notice the difference between spoken and written forms through retelling known stories; compare oral versions with the written text.

5 to retell stories, to give the main points in sequence and to pick out significant incidents.

6 to prepare and retell stories orally, identifying and using some of the more formal features of story language.

7 to use titles, cover pages, pictures and 'blurbs' to predict the content of unfamiliar stories.

8 to compare and contrast stories with a variety of settings, e.g. space, imaginary lands, animal homes.

12 through shared and guided writing to apply phonological, graphic knowledge and sight vocabulary to spell words accurately.

13 to write about significant incidents from known stories.

14 to write stories using simple settings, e.g. based on previous reading.

Planning frame

- Examine the structure of a fantasy story.
- Use the structure to create and language features to write own fantasy story.

How you could plan this unit

Day 1	Day 2	Day 3	Day 4	Day 5
Talk for writing Comparing and contrasting fantasy stories with a variety of settings and characters	**Talk for writing** Sequencing a known fantasy story – *The Paper Bag Princess* by Robert N Munsch or similar (see Resource Page A for introduction)	**Talk for writing** *Developing Characters*	**Reading and writing** *Rewriting Events*	**Reading and writing** Write a simple story plan for own fantasy story

Day 6	Day 7	Day 8	Day 9	Day 10
Reading and writing *Descriptive Language*	**Reading and writing** *Dramatic Language*	**Reading and writing** Writing the end of own fantasy story	**Reading and writing** Creating a front and back cover for own story including title and blurb	**Reading and writing** Evaluating the written outcome using a marking ladder

Developing Characters

Objectives

We will use hot-seating to learn about character. We will talk about the difference between spoken and written language. We will retell stories to the class, using formal story language

You need: *The Paper Bag Princess*, by Robert N Munsch, or similar fantasy story; sequencing work from previous lesson.

Whole class work

- Read the story *The Paper Bag Princess* using different voices for each of the three characters. Demonstrate reading with intonation, paying particular attention to how punctuation affects the way a passage should be read.

- *What type of person is Elizabeth? How did you know this? Which part of the story tells us most about her?*

- Model hot-seating the character of Elizabeth. Explain that you are going to pretend to be Elizabeth and the teaching assistant is going to ask you questions. Answer in role. The children join in asking questions.

> Where do you live? What do you like to do?

Independent, pair or guided work

- Split the class into groups of four. One child in each group takes on the role of the dragon and the remaining three pose questions for the 'dragon' to answer. Some groups may need help in phrasing questions.

- Referring to what they have learned about the characters' personalities, the children decide on a 'voice' for each.

- Using a copy of the sequencing work from the previous lesson as a visual cue, demonstrate how to retell the beginning of the story using appropriate voices for each of the characters as well as making use of more formal story language.

- Using their own sequencing work, the children prepare a retelling of the rest of the story.

Plenary

- Invite a selection of the children to continue the retelling from where you left off. Encourage the use of intonation, a variety in pace and emphasis, and the use of story language. For example, their story ending might be:

> 'You are a toad,' said Elizabeth. They didn't get married at all.

Rewriting Events

Objectives

We will rewrite important events from *The Paper Bag Princess* using story language. We will use capital letters for names and personal titles ('Mr', 'Miss'). We will practise techniques that can help us to spell words accurately

You need: Resource Page C; *The Paper Bag Princess*, by Robert N Munsch, or similar fantasy story; whiteboards and markers (one between two); tape recorder.

Whole class work

- Begin by brainstorming all the significant events from *The Paper Bag Princess*. The children discuss their favourite events with a partner. As they feed back ideas to the rest of the class, prompt them to justify their choices.

- Using one child's suggestion, for example, Elizabeth knocking on the dragon's cave, demonstrate how to retell that particular part of the story, incorporating the use of story language.

- *Can you retell your favourite part of the story in the style it would be written in a book?*

- Invite one child to share their retelling with the class. Demonstrate rewriting that particular event on the board. As you write, take the opportunity to reinforce the use of capital letters for names or personal titles as well as the use of a range of spelling strategies (phonological, graphic, sight vocabulary).

- Discuss your thought process aloud, rehearsing the sentence before writing, making changes to its construction or word choice and explaining why one form or word is preferable to another.

- Using the shared writing, create a class checklist for rewriting significant events from a story (see Resource Page C for ideas).

- The children orally rehearse the first sentence for their own rewriting and use a whiteboard to scribe their ideas. Share examples, prompting the children to identify any errors and improve their use of story language.

Independent, pair or guided work

- Using the class checklist, the children can rewrite their favourite part of the story.

- Lower attaining children could be given the opportunity to record their ideas on to tape.

Plenary

- Select a variety of the children's work so that you have a rewritten version of each significant event from the story.

- Sequence the work so that the events are ordered correctly, then read through all the pieces as if they were a complete version of the book. Discuss the 'finished product' with reference to your class checklist.

Descriptive Language

Objectives

We will use adjectives, similes and powerful verbs to improve our writing, then we will write the beginning of a fantasy story

You need: Resource Pages A–C; whiteboards and pens (one between two).

Whole class work

- Read through the beginning of *The Paper Bag Princess* (Resource Page A) and using the exemplar analysis (Resource Page B), examine what makes a good beginning to a fantasy story.

- Draw attention to the use of adjectives and recall why an author may choose to use them (that is, to give the reader a more detailed picture).

- Ask the children to close their eyes and think carefully about the main character in their story. After one minute allow them to share their descriptions with the rest of the class. Challenge the children to refine their descriptions, revising word choices to create a stronger picture.

- Act as a scribe as the children describe their characters, modelling the use of punctuation and strategies for spelling unfamiliar words (including analogy).

- Explain that to strengthen imagery, an author may sometimes use a simile. Give some examples:

> The wolf's eyes were <u>as</u> large <u>as</u> saucers, his teeth were <u>as</u> sharp <u>as</u> knives.

- Begin a sentence and ask the children to complete the simile:

> The dragon's skin was as green as …
>
> The pixie was as small as …
>
> The ogre was as ugly as …

- Using whiteboards, the children use a simile to describe a character from their story. Share examples and remedy any misconceptions about how similes are constructed.

- Together, compile a class checklist for writing the beginning of a fantasy story (see Resource Page C for ideas).

Independent, pair or guided work

- Using story plans and your class checklist, the children write the beginning of their fantasy story incorporating one simile and at least three adjectives.

Plenary

- Referring back to the text, draw attention to the powerful verb 'smashed'. Explain that a verb is a doing word. ***Here, it is called a 'powerful verb' because it is also helping to describe the way the action is being performed.***

- Selecting a sentence from one of the children's 'beginnings', demonstrate how to incorporate a powerful verb and discuss its effect.

Dramatic Language

Objectives

We will write the middle part of a fantasy story, using onomatopoeia to improve imagery and suspense words and short sentences for dramatic effect

You need: Resource Pages A–C; *The Paper Bag Princess*, by Robert N Munsch, or similar fantasy story; stories with fantasy settings that contain examples of suspense words; whiteboards and pens.

Whole class work

- Using the class checklists from previous lessons, recall the elements that combine to form the middle part of a story: build-up of events; complications; resulting effects.

- Ask the children to identify which events in *The Paper Bag Princess* correspond to which element.

> Build-up – Elizabeth chases dragon.
>
> Complications – Elizabeth tricks the dragon.
>
> Resulting effects – the dragon collapses.

- Reinforce the fact that one event must lead directly on to the next so that the story is easy to follow. The children discuss their story plans with their partner. Share examples.

- Explain that fantasy story writing often involves dramatic events and so authors sometimes use short sentences and/or suspense words.

- Give the children some examples of short sentences and discuss the effect:

> The door slammed. The dragon roared.

- Using *The Paper Bag Princess* in conjunction with other fantasy stories, collect suspense words, for example, 'suddenly', 'all of a sudden', 'without warning'. Using whiteboards, the children scribe one short sentence or a sentence incorporating a suspense word to create dramatic effect.

- Explain that in order to create atmosphere and 'draw in' the reader, an author will often describe sounds and smells. Introduce the term 'onomatopoeia'. As a class brainstorm 'sound' words, such as 'crash', 'crunch', 'splash', 'thud', 'bang!'. Ask the children to think of an event in their story where they could use such a word.

- Create a class checklist for writing the middle of a fantasy story (see Resource Page C for ideas).

Independent, pair or guided work

- Using your class checklist, the children write the middle of their own fantasy story incorporating the use of a short sentence, a suspense word and onomatopoeia.

Plenary

- Share some of the story middles. The children can close their eyes when listening.

- ***Does the writing create an image for the reader? Does it leave the reader wondering what will happen next?***

(Pupil copymaster)

The Paper Bag Princess – story opening

Elizabeth was a beautiful princess. She lived in a castle and had expensive clothes. She was going to marry Prince Ronald.

Unfortunately, a dragon smashed her castle, burned all her clothes with his fiery breath, and carried off Prince Ronald.

from The Paper Bag Princess, *by Robert N Munsch*

(Exemplar analysis)

Example of analysis of *The Paper Bag Princess*

Use of traditional fantasy story characters.

Elizabeth was a beautiful princess. She lived in a castle and had expensive clothes. She was going to marry Prince Ronald.

Unfortunately, a dragon smashed her castle, burned all her clothes with his fiery breath, and carried off Prince Ronald.

from The Paper Bag Princess, *by Robert N Munsch*

Setting is introduced.

Use of adjectives.

Powerful verb.

The beginning makes the reader want to read on.

Exemplar material

Checklists for stories of fantasy worlds

Example of a checklist for summarising a known story ①

- Start your sentences with a capital letter
- Names and titles should also use a capital letter
- Finish each sentence with a full stop
- Segment a word you want to spell into phonemes. Does it look right?
- Your writing must make sense
- Use story language – does your writing sound like a book?

Example of a checklist for planning a fantasy story ②

- Opening includes setting and introduces a fantasy story character: dragon, princess, ogre, pixie, witch, animal
- A series of events build up
- Complications occur
- Resulting events are described
- There is a resolution and an ending

Example of a checklist for the middle of your story ④

- One event leads on to the next
- Use some short sentences to be dramatic
- Use suspense words: 'Suddenly', 'All of a sudden', 'Without warning'
- Use descriptive language: adjectives, expressive verbs, similes, onomatopoeia

Example of a checklist for beginning your story ③

- May use a traditional story start: 'Once upon a time'; 'One day'; 'A long time ago'; 'In a land far away'; 'There once was a …'
- Create setting:
  Time – morning, night, noon, dusk
  Place – castle, mystical land
  Weather – stormy, sunny, cloudy, rainy
- Introduce a limited number of traditional fantasy characters
- Use similes
- Use adjectives
- Use powerful verbs to capture the reader's interest
- Opening should leave the reader wondering what will happen next

Example of a checklist for the end of your story ⑤

- Dilemma is resolved
- Character realises they have been wrong
- There is a happy ending
- Perhaps incorporate a traditional story ending: 'And they all lived happily ever after'; 'And the next day they were married'; 'And from that day to this she never …'

Classworks Literacy Year 1 © Louise Gilbert, Nelson Thornes Ltd 2003

(**Marking ladder**)

Name: _____

Pupil	Objective	Teacher
	My story beginning introduces the character (a traditional fantasy story character).	
	In the middle of my story one event leads to the next.	
	I have used adjectives.	
	I have used simile.	
	I have used suspense words or short sentences for dramatic effect.	
	My story ending resolves the dilemma.	
	I have given my story a happy ending (possibly a traditional story ending).	
	What could I do to improve my story next time?	

Fairy-tale Characters

Outcome

A class book of character profiles

Objectives

Sentence

6 to use the term 'sentence' appropriately to identify sentences in text, i.e. those demarcated by capital letters and full stops.

7 to use capital letters for the personal pronoun 'I', for names and for the start of a sentence.

Text

1 to reinforce and apply their word-level skills through shared and guided reading.

3 to choose and read familiar books with concentration and attention, discuss preferences and give reasons.

6 to identify and discuss a range of story themes, and to collect and compare.

8 to identify and discuss characters, e.g. appearance, behaviour, qualities; to speculate about how they might behave; to discuss how they are described in the text; and to compare characters from different stories or plays.

9 to become aware of character and dialogue, e.g. by role-playing parts when reading aloud stories or plays with others.

15 to build simple profiles of characters from stories read, describing characteristics, appearances, behaviour with pictures, single words, captions, words and sentences from text.

Planning frame

- List strategies authors use to illustrate the personalities of fairy-tale characters.
- Use these strategies to describe different fairy-tale characters.

How you could plan this unit

Day 1	Day 2	Day 3	Day 4	Day 5
Talk for writing Why are characters important? The children identify fairy-tale characters and discuss favourite	Reading	**Reading, writing** The children describe characters' physical features. They draw a picture of a favourite character and add words that describe their physical features	Reading, writing	Reading, writing
	Building a Picture		*Describing Personality*	*Character Riddles*

Day 6	Day 7	Day 8	Day 9	Day 10
Talk for writing Investigate how characters would act in given circumstances (role play)	**Reading, writing** The children design a dinner for a fairy-tale character (reflecting their personality and actions)	Reading, writing	**Reading, writing** Retell fairy tales from the point of view of the 'bad' character	**Reading, writing** Design front cover for class book with title *Fairy-tale character profiles*. Assess outcome using marking ladder
		Alternative Endings		

Building a Picture

Objective

We will discover how authors use words to build up a picture of a character

You need: Resource Pages A–C; a range of traditional tales appropriate for children of differing abilities.

Whole class work

- Revise why characters are important to a story. Explain that they make it more exciting and interesting, particularly when the tale incorporates characters that behave in different ways.

- Fairy tales usually include contrasting characters: bad and good; clever and foolish; rich and poor. Encourage the children to name characters from well-known tales from each category.

- In pairs, prompt the children to discuss how they knew which characters fell into which category. ***How did you decide that the wolf in Little Red Riding Hood was a bad character?*** The children feed back ideas to the whole group.

- Using Resource Page A, examine how the author begins to build up a picture of the character. Explain that firstly, the author has chosen to describe what the character looks like, giving the reader a vivid picture of the beast.

- Explain that authors can use a range of strategies to build up a picture of a character:

  > speech – what the character says or what another character says about them
  >
  > description – what they look like (physical features)
  >
  > actions – what they do
  >
  > interaction – the way the characters behave towards one another

- Using the example on Resource Pages B and C, demonstrate how the author has built up a picture of the wolf without actually describing his physical features.

Independent, pair or guided work

- Using a range of books with traditional fairy tales, encourage the children to identify strategies the author has used to build up a picture of the main character. Write these headings on the board or a flip chart so that the children have access to them.

  > speech
  >
  > description
  >
  > actions
  >
  > interaction

Plenary

- Allow the children time to share their findings. As they discuss the strategies employed by the author, encourage them to refer back to the text for evidence.

- Discuss whether some characters are always portrayed in a certain way, for example, wolves as bad, princesses as good.

Describing Personality

We will describe a character's personality. We will also compare and contrast different characters' personalities

You need: Resource Page D; a range of traditional fairy tales; a picture of the wolf from *Little Red Riding Hood*; paper and crayons; whiteboards and pens.

Whole class work

- Show the children a picture of the wolf from *Little Red Riding Hood*. Reinforcing objectives from the previous lesson, begin by asking the children to brainstorm words that describe the wolf's appearance: hairy, big, grey, and so on.

- Now explain that you want them to describe the wolf's personality. *What type of wolf is he?*

> I think the wolf is 'crafty' because he tricks Red Riding Hood into telling him where she is going.

- In pairs, the children think of three words to describe what the wolf is like. As the children feed back ideas, encourage them to refer to the story for evidence.

- Using the character profiles on Resource Page D, invite selected children to match words that describe personality to the correct fairy-tale character, that is, 'thoughtful' to Red Riding Hood, 'sly' to the wolf, and so on. You can take the opportunity to revise that adjectives are describing words.

- In pairs, the children select a fairy-tale character they know well. Using a whiteboard and pen, they list adjectives describing that particular character's personality. Discuss the children's word choices. *Which words are more powerful/effective?*

- *Think of the characters Snow White and Cinderella. In what ways are their personalities the same and/or different? Can you think of any other fairy-tale characters who are very alike?*

Independent, pair or guided work

- Ask the children to draw a fairy-tale character of their choice in the centre of a piece of paper. Around the outside of the picture, the children write words that describe that character's personality.

Plenary

- Take an example of a child's work. Concealing the picture and character name, ask the rest of the class if they can identify the character. Repeat with different examples.

- Ask the children to consider whether any of the descriptions could have applied to more than one character. If so, what adjectives could be added to clarify and define an individual character?

Character Riddles

Objectives

We will learn to use a capital letter for the personal pronoun 'I'.
We will also use descriptions of a character to form a riddle

You need: Resource Page E; whiteboards and markers (one between two).

Whole class work

- Explain that you are going to pretend to be a character from a well-known fairy tale. The children ask questions to find out which character you are.
  Child: Are you a 'bad' character?
  Teacher: Yes, I am.
  Child: Did you eat Red Riding Hood's Grandmother?
  Teacher: No, I did not.
  Child: Did you fall down the third little pig's chimney?

- Once the children are confident, encourage individuals to 'hot-seat' characters of their own for the class to identify.

- In pairs, one child pretends to be a character from a well-known fairy tale. Giving one fact at a time, they describe themselves in terms of appearance, personality and actions until their partner guesses who they are. For example:

  > I am a girl with blonde hair and blue eyes … I am quite naughty … I like to eat porridge …

- Demonstrate how to write a 'guess the character' riddle (see Resource Page E, example 3), drawing the children's attention to the use of a capital letter for the pronoun 'I'.

- Compile a class checklist for writing a riddle (see Resource Page E for ideas).

- The children decide on a character for their own 'Guess who?' Each child scribes ideas on to a whiteboard, orally rehearsing the sentence prior to writing. Share some examples, taking the opportunity to reinforce a range of spelling strategies.

Independent, pair or guided work

- Each child writes their own 'Guess who?' fairy-tale character riddle.

Plenary

- The children share their riddles. Other members of the class guess the fairy-tale character.

- Discuss which pieces of information were most useful in identifying the characters.

Alternative Endings

Objective

We will create a 'Wanted' poster incorporating a character description

You need: Resource Page E; a copy of *Little Red Riding Hood*; wolf mask or wolf costume (not essential), or picture of the wolf; Post-it™ notes.

Whole class work

- Read through the story of *Little Red Riding Hood*, preferably in big book format.

- Discuss any alternative endings to the story that the children may have heard, for example, the wolf escapes; the wolf eats Little Red Riding Hood; the woodcutter kills the wolf, and so on. *Why do some versions have different endings?* Remind the children that traditional fairy tales have been passed from generation to generation by word of mouth.

- Ask the children to discuss their own ideas on how the story should end. Invite them to share their alternative endings.

- Select one child's alternative ending in which the wolf escapes. Explain that in order to catch the wolf the local police force have decided to put up 'Wanted' posters. Explain that the posters must incorporate a detailed description.

- Invite one child to stand in front of the class to play the part of the wolf. (If possible provide a simple mask or wolf costume.) Encourage the other children to suggest words that describe the wolf's physical features, his personality and his actions, for example:

| large | grey | hairy | sly | crafty | likes scaring people |

These words or phrases can be written on Post-it™ notes and stuck on to 'the wolf'.

- Using example 4, Resource Page E, demonstrate how to incorporate the ideas into a 'Wanted' poster.

- Create a class checklist to assist the children in their independent work (see Resource Page E for ideas).

Independent, pair or guided work

- Using the checklist created in whole class work, the children create a 'Wanted' poster to assist in the capture of a villainous fairy-tale character.

- Less able children could use the example of the wolf whilst more able children could select an alternative character.

Plenary

- Ask the children to share their work. Challenge the rest of the class to identify the character from their description. *Why did you use these words/this picture?*

- Did any children have any of the same words for a different character? If so, what differentiated the posters/characters?

The Beast with a Thousand Teeth

A long time ago, in a land far away, the most terrible beast that ever lived roamed the countryside. It had four eyes, six legs and a thousand teeth. In the morning it would gobble up men as they went to work in the fields. In the afternoon it would break into lonely farms and eat up mothers and children as they sat down to lunch, and at night it would stalk the streets of towns, looking for its supper.

Terry Jones

(Exemplar material)

The Three Little Pigs

Once upon a time there was a mother pig who had three little pigs.

The three little pigs grew so big that their mother said to them, 'You are too big to live here any longer. You must go and build a house for yourselves. But take care that the wolf does not catch you.'

The three little pigs set off. 'We will take care that the wolf does not catch us,' they said.

Soon they met a man who was carrying some straw. 'Please will you give me some straw?' asked the first little pig. 'I want to build a house for myself.'

'Yes,' said the man and he gave the first little pig some straw.

Then the first little pig built himself a house of straw. He was very pleased with his house. He said, 'Now the wolf won't catch me and eat me.'

'I shall build a stronger house than yours,' said the second little pig.

'I shall build a stronger house than yours, too,' said the third little pig.

The second little pig and the third little pig went along the road. Soon they met a man who was carrying some sticks.

'Please will you give me some sticks?' asked the second little pig. 'I want to build a house for myself.'

'Yes,' said the man and he gave the second little pig some sticks.

Then the second little pig built himself a house of sticks. It was stronger than the house of straw. The second little pig was very pleased with his house. He said, 'Now the wolf won't catch me and eat me.'

'I shall build a stronger house than yours,' said the third little pig.

The third little pig walked on along the road, by himself. Soon he met a man who was carrying some bricks.

'Please will you give me some bricks?' asked the third little pig. 'I want to build a house for myself.'

'Yes,' said the man and he gave the third little pig some bricks.

Then the third little pig built himself a house of bricks.

The next day the wolf came along the road. He came to the house built of straw which the first little pig had built.

When the first little pig saw the wolf coming, he ran inside his house and shut the door.

The wolf knocked on the door and said, 'Little pig, little pig, let me come in.'

'No, no,' said the little pig. 'By the hair of my chinny chin chin, I will not let you come in.'

'Then I'll huff and I'll puff and I'll blow your house in,' said the wolf.

So he huffed and he puffed and he huffed and he puffed. The house of straw fell down and the wolf ate up the first little pig.

Ladybird Easy Reading

(Exemplar analysis)

Example of analysis of *The Three Little Pigs*

Once upon a time there was a mother pig who had three little pigs.

The three little pigs grew so big that their mother said to them, 'You are too big to live here any longer. You must go and build a house for yourselves. But take care that the wolf does not catch you.'

Other characters describing the wolf through speech.

The three little pigs set off. 'We will take care that the wolf does not catch us,' they said.

Soon they met a man who was carrying some straw. 'Please will you give me some straw?' asked the first little pig. 'I want to build a house for myself.'

'Yes,' said the man and he gave the first little pig some straw.

Then the first little pig built himself a house of straw. He was very pleased with his house. He said, 'Now the wolf won't catch me and eat me.'

Other characters' actions help build up a picture of the wolf.

'I shall build a stronger house than yours,' said the second little pig.

'I shall build a stronger house than yours, too,' said the third little pig.

The second little pig and the third little pig went along the road. Soon they met a man who was carrying some sticks.

'Please will you give me some sticks?' asked the second little pig. 'I want to build a house for myself.'

'Yes,' said the man and he gave the second little pig some sticks.

Then the second little pig built himself a house of sticks. It was stronger than the house of straw. The second little pig was very pleased with his house. He said, 'Now the wolf won't catch me and eat me.'

'I shall build a stronger house than yours,' said the third little pig.

The third little pig walked on along the road, by himself. Soon he met a man who was carrying some bricks.

'Please will you give me some bricks?' asked the third little pig. 'I want to build a house for myself.'

'Yes,' said the man and he gave the third little pig some bricks.

The wolf adding to his own description through speech.

Then the third little pig built himself a house of bricks.

The next day the wolf came along the road. He came to the house built of straw which the first little pig had built.

When the first little pig saw the wolf coming, he ran inside his house and shut the door.

The wolf knocked on the door and said, 'Little pig, little pig, let me come in.'

'No, no,' said the little pig. 'By the hair of my chinny chin chin, I will not let you come in.'

Describing the wolf's actions assists the reader in building a picture of his character.

'Then I'll huff and I'll puff and I'll blow your house in,' said the wolf.

So he huffed and he puffed and he huffed and he puffed. The house of straw fell down and the wolf ate up the first little pig.

Ladybird Easy Reading

Pupil copymaster

Character profiles

caring   thoughtful   sneaky

sly   wicked   kind

trusting   honest   naughty

crafty   hard-working

(Exemplar material)

Checklists and models for fairy-tale characters

Example of a checklist for writing a character riddle

- Use a capital letter for the word 'I'

- Describe a physical feature

- Describe the character's personality

- Describe something the character did in the fairy tale (an action) – blowing a house down, breaking Baby Bear's chair

- Use full stops at the end of each sentence

Example of a checklist for creating a 'Wanted' poster

- A villainous fairy-tale character is selected

- The character is named on the poster (Mr Big Bad Wolf, Miss Goldilocks)

- The poster incorporates a suitable picture of the villain

- The poster details why the character is wanted

- The poster describes:
  - the character's physical features
  - their personality
  - their actions

- A reward is advertised

Model of a character riddle

WHO AM I?

- I have big ears and a hairy coat

- I am crafty and sly

- I enjoy eating grannies and putting on their clothes

- I don't like woodcutters

Model of a 'Wanted' poster

WANTED

Mr Big Bad Wolf

For attempting to eat Little Red Riding Hood and her old Granny.

£100 REWARD

The Big Bad Wolf is described as being large, grey and hairy. He is very crafty and shows great delight in scaring old ladies and young girls.

WARNING: This wolf is extremely dangerous. If you see him, call the police immediately.

(Marking ladder)

Name: _____

Pupil	Objective	Teacher
	I have described physical features accurately and used of adjectives.	
	I have chosen appropriate words to describe a character's personality.	
	I have used a capital letter for the personal pronoun 'I'.	
	I can refer back to the text for evidence.	
	What could I do to improve my profile next time?	

Rhymes with a Pattern

 **Outcome**

A class anthology of rhymes modelled on those read

Objectives

Sentence

1 to expect written text to make sense and to check for sense if it does not.

3 to draw on grammatical awareness, to read with appropriate expression and intonation, e.g. in reading to others, or to dolls, puppets.

5 to recognise full stops and capital letters when reading, and name them correctly.

Text

1 to reinforce and apply their word-level skills through shared and guided reading.

4 to read familiar, simple stories and poems independently, to point while reading and make correspondence between words said and read.

6 to recite stories and rhymes with predictable and repeating patterns, extemporising on patterns orally by substituting words and phrases, extending patterns, inventing patterns and playing with rhyme.

8 through shared and guided writing to apply phonological, graphic knowledge and sight vocabulary to spell words accurately.

10 to use rhymes and patterned stories as models for their own writing.

Planning frame

● Identify repetitive patterns in rhyme.

● Use patterns to create individual pieces of work.

Note

● For the purposes of this unit, the definitions for 'rhyme' and 'poem' are broadly interchangeable. However: rhyme = verse composition with words that rhyme; poem = verse composition, may or may not have words that rhyme.

How you could plan this unit

Day 1	Day 2	Day 3	Day 4	Day 5
Collecting and reading Rhymes with predictable and repetitive patterns	Reading	**Reading** Sequencing rhymes using predictable and repetitive patterns. Re-sequencing cut-up rhymes	Writing	Reading and writing
	Ten Tired Tigers		*Using Numbers*	*Using Alliteration*

Day 6	Day 7	Day 8
Reading and writing	**Reading and writing** Redrafting one of the poems written during the unit using ICT	**Reading** Critical evaluation of poems. Create a class anthology. Use marking ladder
Rhyme Strings		

Ten Tired Tigers

Objectives

We will think about why poets use repetitive patterns and learn how to spot them in a rhyme

You need: Resource Pages A–C and H.

Whole class work

- Read *Ten Tired Tigers* (Resource Page A). Discuss the children's immediate response to the rhyme. ***Did you enjoy listening to it? Which was your favourite part and why?***

- Reread the rhyme, encouraging the children to join in. Once finished, ask them to consider why they found it easy to recall. Steer towards the poet's use of a predictable pattern.

- Explain that poets use repetitive or predictable patterns to make their rhymes more memorable and more enjoyable to read.

- Giving time to reflect on the rhyme, invite the children to identify the repetitive or predictable patterns within the text (see Resource Page B). Allow the children to share their ideas.

- Incorporate the points identified into a class checklist of patterns used by poets to create rhymes (see Resource Page H for ideas).

- Cover up the rhyme. Work as a group to recite the rhyme using the repetitive pattern identified as a scaffold. Question the children throughout the recitation to develop their understanding. ***What will the next line begin with? How do you know? What type of word will be next?***

Independent, pair or guided work

- Using a copy of the well-known rhyme *One, Two, Buckle My Shoe* (Resource Page C), the children read through the rhyme and then identify the repetitive patterns contained within it.

- The children record the patterns they identify in their own way, for example, highlighting in different colours, rewriting a relevant line, and so on.

Plenary

- Allow the children time to share the patterns they identified. Ensure all patterns have been discussed.

- Reread the last line in the poem *Ten Tired Tigers*. ***How does the last line still reflect the repetitive/predictable pattern?*** Explain that in this case the poet had to change some elements of the pattern in order to draw the rhyme to a close.

- Reread the rhyme together with pace and expression.

Using Numbers

Objectives

We will write a simple number rhyme with a repetitive pattern and choose adjectives to describe animals

You need: Resource Pages G and H; variety of repetitive number rhymes; pictures of zoo animals; whiteboards and pens.

Whole class work

- Reread a range of the number rhymes containing predictable/repetitive patterns collated during previous lessons. As you read, extemporise on the patterns, adding any additional ones identified in checklist 1 (Resource Page H).

- Explain that today the children are going to learn how poets create a number rhyme with a predictable and repetitive pattern. *The rhyme is called* **Down at the Zoo** *(see Resource Page G for example) and is going to use numbers in ascending order as well as an animal and a word to describe it, as in* **Ten Tired Tigers.**

- On a flip chart, write the title and begin the poem with the word 'One'. Explain that the next two words will be linked: the third word being the name of an animal, the second an adjective to describe it.

- Hold up a picture of a zoo animal (for example, an elephant). In pairs, the children think of a word that describes that creature. Each pair scribe their ideas on to a whiteboard. Share some examples, asking the children to discuss their choice of word. *Which words are more suitable than others and why?*

- Use one of the children's ideas to complete the first line.

> One FAT elephant

  Continue selecting new animals and adjectives until the third line is complete.

- Explain that to make the poem more interesting you are going to add another repetitive pattern. Every fourth line will be identical rather like a chorus in a song. Continue to share-write the poem up to the end of the second verse.

Independent, pair or guided work

- Using the model from the shared session, the children create two further verses.

Plenary

- Invite selected children to share their additional verses. *Have the repetitive and predictable patterns been adhered to? Have appropriate adjectives been selected?*

- Show one picture of a zoo animal. Sitting in a circle, the children list adjectives to describe that animal. *How many appropriate words can we collect?*

Using Alliteration

Objective

We will write a repetitive number rhyme that uses alliteration

You need: Resource Pages D and E; pictures of animals not mentioned in the rhyme (for example, spider, shark, elephant).

Whole class work

- Read *Zoo Dream* (Resource Page D) to the children.

- Conceal the text and ask the children to recall what each group of animals was doing.

  > 'The crocodiles were … clapping'
  > 'The monkeys were … marching'

- The children identify why the words were so easy to recall. Introduce the word 'alliteration'.

- To assist the children in identifying and creating alliteration, begin an alliterative sentence for them to complete.

  > Silly Sally saw a ——————
  >
  > Alex Ant ate an ——————

- In pairs, the children analyse the poem, identifying the repetitive and predictable patterns:
  - use of an introductory verse before repetitive pattern begins
  - numbers used in descending order
  - second word in each line is an animal (plural used where necessary)
  - third word ends in 'ing' and describes what the animals are doing
  - use of alliteration.

- Reinforcing the use of alliteration and the use of 'ing', hold up a picture of a new animal, for example, a spider. Discuss which words might be suitable to describe what the spiders could be doing – 'singing', 'stamping', 'spinning', and so on.

- Explain that they are going to create their own version of the rhyme using the existing predictable/repetitive patterns. Demonstrate how to enter the name of a new animal group and an appropriate word to describe what they are doing, for example, 'Ten *spiders singing*'.

Independent, pair or guided work

- Using the blank frame (Resource Page E) encourage the children to complete an alternative version of the rhyme using alliteration.

Plenary

- Invite selected children to share their work. As a class, assess their use of the repetitive pattern. *Have they used alliteration? Does the last word in each line end in 'ing'?*

- Discuss whether the alliteration can be further improved by using the whole of the consonant blend, where possible, as opposed to simply the initial letter, for example, *cr*ocodiles *cr*unching as opposed to *cl*apping, *sn*akes *sn*apping as opposed to *sl*eeping.

Rhyme Strings

Objectives

We will create some rhyme strings. We will also write a poem with a rhyming pattern

You need: Resource Page F; magnetic letters.

Whole class work

- Using magnetic letters, display the word 'hen'. As a class, blend the phonemes together to read the word, then ask a child to remove the initial letter 'h' and replace it with an alternative onset ('p', 't', 'd' or 'm') to create a new word.

- Read the new word then change the first letter to create yet another. List the words that have been created. *What do you notice?*

- If necessary, discuss what is meant by the term 'rhyme'. Explain that you have to listen for matching sounds – for example, 'pour' and 'door'. Matching letters do not necessarily rhyme – 'bone', 'one'.

- With the children sitting in a circle, begin by selecting a simple CVC word, for example, 'cat', 'pan' or 'rug'. Each child adds a rhyming word, creating a rhyme string.

- Read *Caribbean Counting Rhyme* (Resource Page F). Having given time to reflect on the text, encourage the children to identify the repetitive/predictable patterns within it.

> Numbers ascend with each verse
>
> First line of each verse repeats the number word, separated with the word 'by' – 'one by one' and so on
>
> First and second line of each verse is identical
>
> Last words in lines 2 and 4 of each verse rhyme

- Reread the first verse and then create a rhyme string for the word 'one'. Selecting one of the alternative rhyming words, for example, 'bun' or 'fun', substitute the last two lines to create an alternative verse:

> One by one
> one by <u>one</u>
> making sandcastles
> is lots of <u>fun</u>.

Independent, pair or guided work

- Using *Caribbean Counting Rhyme*, encourage the children to substitute the last two lines of each verse to create a new rhyme. They must ensure that the last word in lines 2 and 4 of each verse rhyme.

Plenary

- The children share their poems. *How many alternative rhyming words have been used for each verse?*

Pupil copymaster

Ten Tired Tigers

Ten tired tigers all fast asleep.

Twenty tiny turtles creep, creep, creep.

Thirty noisy thrushes chatter in a tree.

Forty silver fishes swim in the sea.

Fifty naughty frogs jump in a hat.

Clap your hands together and they'll

Scat! Scat! Scat!

David Orme

(Exemplar analysis)

Example of analysis of *Ten Tired Tigers*

The first word in each line is a number word that increases by 10 each time.

Ten tired tigers all fast asleep.

Twenty tiny turtles creep, creep, creep.

Thirty noisy thrushes chatter in a tree.

Forty silver fishes swim in the sea.

Fifty naughty frogs jump in a hat.

Clap your hands together and they'll

Scat! Scat! Scat!

David Orme

The second and third words in each line are linked: the third names an animal, the second is an adjective describing it.

The last words in each pair of lines rhyme.

The last three or four words in each line describe what the animals are doing.

One, Two, Buckle My Shoe

One, two,

buckle my shoe.

Three, four,

knock at the door.

Five, six,

pick up sticks.

Seven, eight,

lay them straight.

Nine, ten,

a big fat hen.

Classworks Literacy Year 1 © Louise Gilbert, Nelson Thornes Ltd 2003

(Pupil copymaster)

Zoo Dream

I dreamed I went to the zoo one day.

All the animals came out to play.

There were

Ten whales whistling,

Nine hippos hopping,

Eight monkeys marching,

Seven lions laughing,

Six snakes skipping,

Five donkeys dancing,

Four crocodiles clapping,

Three rhinos roaring,

Two giraffes giggling

And one seal snoring!

John Foster

(Pupil copymaster)

Zoo Dream writing frame

_____ 's Zoo Dream

I dreamed I went to the zoo one day.

All the animals came out to play.

There were

Ten _____ _____,

Nine _____ _____,

Eight _____ _____,

Seven _____ _____,

Six _____ _____,

Five _____ _____,

Four _____ _____,

Three _____ _____,

Two _____ _____

And _____ _____!

(**Pupil copymaster**)

Caribbean Counting Rhyme

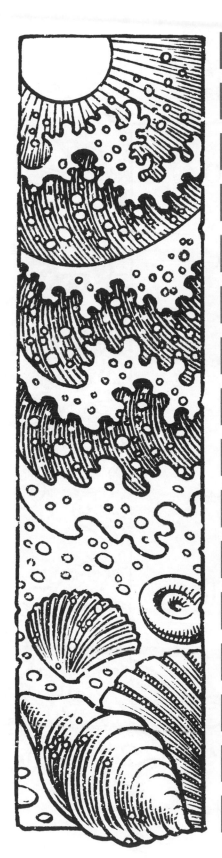

One by one
one by one
waves are dancing
in the sun.

Two by two
Two by two
Seashells pink
And purply-blue.

Three by three
Three by three
Big boats
Putting out to sea.

Four by four
Four by four
Children fishing
On the shore.

Five by five
Five by five
Little walking
Fish arrive.

Pamela Mordecai

Classworks Literacy Year 1 © Louise Gilbert, Nelson Thornes Ltd 2003

Exemplar material

Example of a model of a rhyme with pattern

DOWN AT THE ZOO

One fat elephant,

Two wise owls,

Three slippery snakes,

Down at the zoo.

Four sneaky leopards,

Five stripy tigers,

Six snapping crocodiles,

Down at the zoo.

Classworks Literacy Year 1 © Louise Gilbert, Nelson Thornes Ltd 2003

(Exemplar material)

Checklist for rhymes with a pattern

- Numbers: in ascending or descending order by a given amount (in ones, twos, tens, and so on)

- Rhyme: either each pair of lines or every other line

- Repetition of word type: for example, the name of an animal being the third word on each line

- Words may be linked to one another: for example, the second word in each line describes the animal

Marking ladder

Name: _____

Pupil	Objective	Teacher
	Our anthology includes a number poem using numbers in ascending or descending order.	
	It includes a poem using rhyme.	
	It includes a poem using alliteration.	
	It includes a poem incorporating a 'chorus' or repeated line.	
	It includes a poem using describing words.	
	Our anthology uses correct punctuation.	
	Our writing makes sense.	
	What could we do to improve our anthology next time?	

Lists and Captions

Outcome

Lists and captions for a class display

Objectives

Sentence

2 to use awareness of the grammar of a sentence to decipher new or unfamiliar words, e.g. predict text from the grammar, read on, leave a gap and reread.

4 to write captions and simple sentences, and to reread, recognising whether or not they make sense, e.g. missing words, wrong word order.

5 to recognise full stops and capital letters when reading, and name them correctly.

6 to begin using the term 'sentence' to identify sentences in text.

7 [be taught] that a line of writing is not necessarily the same as a sentence.

Text

2 to use phonological, contextual, grammatical and graphic knowledge to work out, predict and check the meanings of unfamiliar words and to make sense of what they read.

12 to read and use captions, e.g. labels around the school, on equipment.

14 to write captions for their own work, e.g. for display, in class books.

15 to make simple lists for planning, reminding, etc.

Planning frame

- Understand how and why lists are composed.
- Understand why captions are useful and how they are composed.
- Write own lists and captions.

How you could plan this unit

Day 1	Day 2	Day 3	Day 4	Day 5
Talk for writing Identifying and reading lists and captions around the classroom/school	Reading, writing	Reading, writing	Reading, writing	Reading, writing
	A List of Toys	*Sorting into Categories*	*Writing a Caption*	*Longer Captions*

A List of Toys

Objectives

We will find out what a list is and why lists are used, then we will write a simple list

You need: Resource Pages A and H; 30 small pieces of paper (approx 10cm x 5cm); pencils; A3 sheet of coloured sugar paper; strips of paper for list writing.

Whole class work

- Begin by revising, *What is a list and when do we use one?* Explain that lists are often used for reminding (oneself or others), for planning or for presenting information clearly.

- Brainstorm all the places the children have seen lists being used.

- Show the shopping list (Resource Page A). Having read through the list together, invite the children to discuss what they notice about the way it is written:

- Compile the findings into a class checklist for writing simple lists (see Resource Page H for ideas).

> Start each new item on a new line (one underneath the other)
>
> No need for punctuation
>
> No need for full sentences

- Explain that as a class they are going to make a display about toys. The display will incorporate pictures, lists and captions as a way of presenting information on a given subject.

- You could link this to QCA History Unit 1, 'How are our toys different from those in the past?'

- Reinforce the way a list is written by compiling a list of 'Our Favourite Toys'. Give each child a small piece of paper and a pencil and ask them to write the name of one favourite toy: Lego, toy lion, bicycle, and so on. Assemble the pieces of paper into a list by gluing them one below another on to a large sheet of paper.

Independent, pair or guided work

- Using strips of paper with the heading 'My Toys', encourage the children to write words one below the other, to compile a list of all the toys they have at home.

Plenary

- Referring to the class checklist created in whole class work, the children swap lists with a partner and assess whether the features identified during the shared session have been incorporated.

- Sitting in a circle, play 'I went to the toy shop and bought ...'. Each child lists, in order, the toys mentioned by previous members of the group and then adds a new idea of their own. *How many toys can we list in the correct order?*

Sorting into Categories

Objective

We will use lists to organise and present information

You need: Resource Page H; a range of children's toys – water toys, wheeled toys, puzzles, wind toys, toy animals, construction toys; strips of paper for writing lists; A4 card; A3 paper.

Whole class work

- Explain that lists can be used to sort and present information to others clearly.

- The children sit in a circle. Put a range of different toys in the centre. Allow a few minutes for the children to discuss the toys with a partner.

- Select one pair to begin to sort the toys in any way they feel appropriate. As they sort, encourage the children to discuss the categories by which the toys have been sorted.

- Once the pair has completed categorising the toys, allow other children to discuss alternative possibilities in terms of grouping.

- As a class, decide on the most appropriate headings by which the toys can be sorted and write each heading on to a separate piece of A4 card, for example:

| water toys | wheeled toys | puzzles | wind toys | toy animals |

- Group the class (mixed ability) so each group has a different heading to work with. The children then select toys that fall into that category and compile a list on A3 paper.

- Allow time for each group to read through their list. ***Are there any toys that belonged in more than one list?*** Reinforce the ways lists should be written by referring to checklist 1 (Resource Page H).

Independent, pair or guided work

- Using the list of 'My Toys' from the previous lesson, the children choose suitable categories for their own toys (up to six categories).

- Using strips of paper, the children divide their list into new lists that sort their toys into different categories.

Plenary

- Selecting several children to share their lists, invite them to discuss how they categorised their toys. Encourage the children to analyse how the lists created during today's lesson assist readers in accessing information quickly.

- Asking one child to use the lists created by someone else, challenge them to locate specific information:

> Find a toy that has four wheels.
> Find a toy that floats.

109

Writing a Caption

Objective

We will write simple captions

You need: Resource Pages B–E and H; a toy from the classroom.

Whole class work

- Review how the children have used lists to organise and present information about their toys. Explain that another way of conveying information is by using captions.

- Show the children Resource Page B. Read through the caption together and examine the picture before analysing the way the caption is written (see Resource Page C for ideas). Discuss the language and use of a picture.

- Show the children Resource Page D. In pairs, the children read and analyse the text independently to decide whether the features of caption writing identified previously apply.

- Work as a group to create a class checklist for writing captions (see Resource Page H for ideas).

- Show the children a spinning top (or the picture, Resource Page E). Pass the toy/picture around the group, allowing time to explore and discuss in detail. **What do you think it is made of? What does it do? Who might use it? How is it decorated?**

- Explain that they are now going to draw their own picture of a toy and write a caption to go with it. Demonstrate by drawing a picture of the top, reinforcing the importance of clarity. Remind the children that their first sentence must quickly and clearly tell the reader what the object is. Ask them to suggest how the caption might start. Select a simple, clear example to scribe.

Independent, pair or guided work

- The children draw a detailed and clear picture of their favourite toy.

- They write the first short sentence of their caption that tells the reader what the toy is.

Plenary

- Invite several children to share their work, then encourage the rest of the class to assess how well they have incorporated the features of caption writing identified during the shared session, using the class checklist.

- Hold up a different toy and ask the children to quickly think of an initial sentence for a caption – ensure that suggestions use full sentences. Discuss the captions they suggest. **Which are most effective and why?**

Longer Captions

Objectives

We will write more captions, this time including more detail. We will also learn that a sentence is not always the same as a line of writing

You need: Resource Pages B, D and F–I; a bucket and spade; whiteboards and pens.

Whole class work

- Reread *Lego* and *Kites* (Resource Pages B and D). Ask the children to recall the key features of caption writing (see checklist 2, Resource Page H, and your class checklist from the previous lesson).

- Explain that today's lesson will focus on writing the second sentence in a caption – the sentence that gives the reader more information.

- Display a bucket and spade and invite the children to discuss any experiences they have of using them. *Where would you use them? Who would use them? What would you use them for?*

- Show the children Resource Page F and explain that the caption needs completing. *There is a a clear picture and a short first sentence, but we need a second, longer sentence giving additional information.*

- In pairs, the children use their existing knowledge about buckets and spades to create a sentence to complete the caption.

- Allow time for the children to share their ideas. Encourage them to give their ideas in full sentences. Select a clear example and model how to write the sentence, thus completing the caption (see Resource Page G).

- As you write, draw attention to the use of capital letters and full stops. Draw particular attention to the fact that a sentence is not necessarily the same as a line of writing. The full stop should not come until the end of the idea/sentence.

- Using whiteboards, the children refine then scribe their own sentences to complete the caption. Prompt the children to discuss the strategies they used to spell unfamiliar words: counting phonemes, analogy, and so on.

Independent, pair or guided work

- Continuing with the work begun in the previous lesson, the children complete their caption about a toy by adding a second longer sentence that gives additional information.

Plenary

- Using the marking ladder (Resource Page I), encourage the children to share, then self-evaluate their work. The children can use a response sandwich to guide the evaluations: one good thing, one idea for improvement, a second good thing.

Pupil copymaster

Shopping list

Shopping

4 bananas

milk

eggs

sugar

butter

crisps (salt and vinegar)

bread

sweets

orange squash

6 apples

(**Pupil copymaster**)

Lego

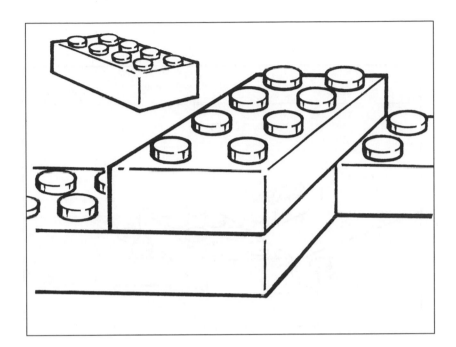

Lego is a construction toy. It can be put together to build a model then taken apart again.

(Exemplar analysis)

Example of analysis of 'Lego' page

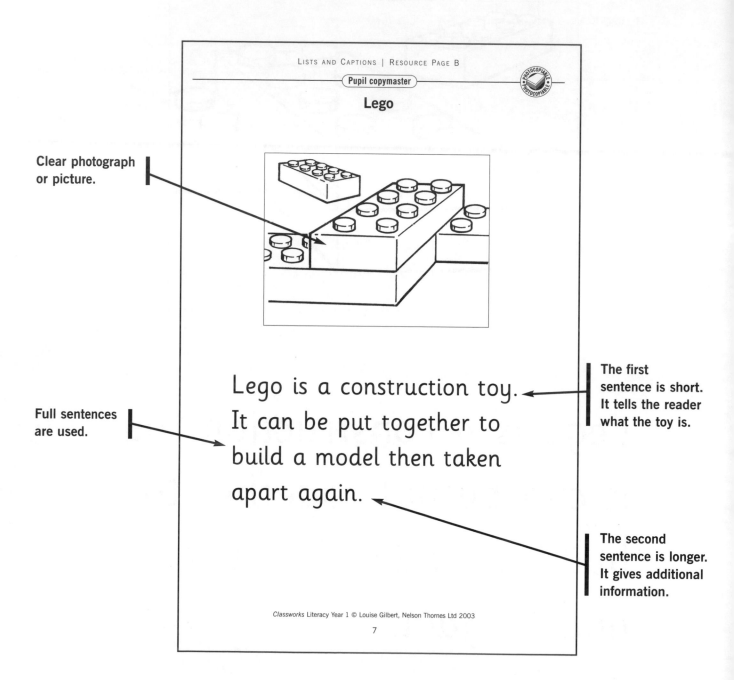

(Pupil copymaster)

Lego

Clear photograph or picture.

Full sentences are used.

Lego is a construction toy. It can be put together to build a model then taken apart again.

The first sentence is short. It tells the reader what the toy is.

The second sentence is longer. It gives additional information.

Classworks Literacy Year 1 © Louise Gilbert, Nelson Thornes Ltd 2003

7

Pupil copymaster

Kites

Kites are used all around the world.
The first kites were made in China from thin paper or silk.

(Pupil copymaster)

A spinning top

(**Pupil copymaster**)

Writing frame

Buckets and spades can be great fun.

Classworks Literacy Year 1 © Louise Gilbert, Nelson Thornes Ltd 2003

(**Pupil copymaster**)

Buckets and spades

Buckets and spades can be great fun. At the seaside you can make castles by filling the buckets with wet sand and turning them over.

(Exemplar material)

Checklists for lists and captions

Example of a checklist for writing a simple list	**Example of a checklist for writing a caption**

Example of a checklist for writing a simple list ①

- List words/items one beneath the other, with each new item on a new line

- No punctuation should be used

- Do not use full sentences. Any additional information can be given in note form, for example, quantity, colour, type

Example of a checklist for writing a caption ②

- Use a clear picture/photograph to attract the reader

- Keep the first sentence short. State what the object is, clearly and concisely

- Make the second sentence longer. Give more information about the object

(**Marking ladder**)

Name: _____

Pupil	Objective	Teacher
	My list is written with each item on a new line, one beneath the other.	
	My list is not written in full sentences.	
	My list uses no punctuation.	
	My caption includes a clear picture.	
	My first sentence tells the reader what the object is.	
	My second sentence gives more information.	
	What could I do to improve my work next time?	

Recount of a Class Visit

Outcome

Recount of a visit to the Post Office, using temporal connectives

Objectives

Sentence

1 to expect reading to make sense and check if it does not.

2 to use awareness of the grammar of a sentence to decipher new or unfamiliar words, e.g. predict text from the grammar, read on, leave a gap and reread.

4 [be taught] about word order, e.g. by re-ordering sentences, predicting words from previous text, grouping a range of words that might 'fit', and discussing the reasons why.

6 through reading and writing, to reinforce knowledge of the term 'sentence' from previous terms.

7 to add question marks to questions.

Text

17 to recognise that non-fiction books on similar themes can give different information and present similar information in different ways.

18 to read recounts and begin to recognise generic structure, e.g. ordered sequence of events, use of words like 'first', 'next', 'after', 'when'.

19 to identify simple questions and use text to find answers. To locate parts of text that give particular information including labelled diagrams and charts, e.g. 'parts of a car', 'what pets eat', 'clothes that keep us warm'.

20 to write simple recounts linked to topics of interest/study or to personal experience, using the language of texts read as models for own writing. Make group/class books, e.g. 'our day at school', 'our trip to...'.

21 to use the language and features of non-fiction texts, e.g. labelled diagrams, captions for pictures, to make class books e.g. 'What We Know About...', 'Our Pets'.

22 to write own questions prior to reading for information and to record answers, e.g. as lists, a completed chart, extended captions for display, a fact file on IT.

Planning frame

- Write questions, read a recount, then create own recount.

How you could plan this unit

Day 1	Day 2	Day 3	Day 4	Day 5
Talk for writing Visit to a Post Office. Take photographs of the route and visit. Develop photos before Day 3	**Talk for writing/writing**	**Reading and writing**	**Reading and writing**	**Reading and writing**
	Questions and Answers	*Chronological Order*	*Setting the Scene*	*Amusing Events and Conclusion*

121

Questions and Answers

Objectives

We will write and answer simple questions, using a question mark correctly. We will locate information in a non-fiction text

You need: Resource Pages A and D; whiteboards and pens; A4 paper (1 per child); strips of paper (4 per child); non-fiction text about the Post Office or post.

Whole class work

- Begin by discussing the visit in general terms. *Which part of the trip was your favourite? Why? What was the most interesting piece of information you found out?*

- Show the children the question hand (Resource Page A). Explain that the hand is a good way of remembering important question words. Demonstrate how each finger represents a different word beginning with 'w' and the palm represents the word 'how'.

- Using the question hand as an aid, the children compose one question about the visit to ask their response partner. The partners should answer.

- Prompt each pair to share their questions and answers and, as a class, categorise each under the question word used. Discuss each question word in turn. *What sort of information can you find out by using it? What sort of answer would you expect?*

- Begin to compile a list of key words related to the visit: 'post office', 'envelope', 'sorting office', 'post box', 'stamp', 'address', 'postman/woman'.

- Select one key word and one question word, for example, 'address' and 'why'. The children compose then scribe a suitable question using their whiteboards.

> Why do you write an address on an envelope?

- Invite the children to swap boards and read their partner's question, then write the answer underneath, for example:

> So the postman knows where to take it.

- Share some questions and answers. Draw attention to the use of a question mark.

- Create a checklist for writing questions (see Resource Page D for ideas).

Independent, pair or guided work

- Using the question hand, the list of key words and the checklist as a support, the children write four questions about the visit on their whiteboards, using different question words. They then write the answers on four separate strips of paper.

Plenary

- Using one child's work, begin by reading all four questions and then the four answers in random order. The children match the answers to the questions.

- Using your checklist, encourage the children to assess whether the key features of writing questions have been suitably incorporated into their work.

- *Did anyone write a question you don't know the answer to?* Demonstrate how to locate specific information in the non-fiction text. (You may wish to prepare some example questions that can be answered by the text.)

Chronological Order

Objective

We will order a sequence of events, using temporal connectives

You need: Resource Pages B and D; photographs taken during the visit; Post-it™ notes.

Whole class work

- Begin by examining the photographs taken during the visit (in random order). Encourage the children to identify all the different events that took place.

- *Over the next few days you are going to write a recount – the 'story' of your visit for others to read.*

- Explain that recounts are written in chronological order and discuss what is meant by this term. *Why do you think it is important that recounts are written in chronological order?*

- As a class, sequence the photographs chronologically.

- Explain that there are special words, called temporal (or time) connectives, which will assist them in writing their recount in chronological order.

- Read the sample recount about a visit to the police station (Resource Page B). Assist the children in identifying the temporal connectives: 'first', 'then', 'next', 'finally'. Write each on a separate Post-it™, as well as any other such connectives the children can think of, for example, 'lastly', 'after' and so on.

- Looking at the first of the sequenced photographs, discuss which of the temporal connectives could be used when recounting this part of the story ('first'/'firstly'). Continue through each of the sequenced photographs, attaching an appropriate temporal connective.

- Using the sequenced photographs and their appropriate temporal connective, invite several children to recount the visit orally.

Independent, pair or guided work

- Invite the children to draw a series of up to four clear pictures, linked by arrows, to represent the elements of their visit, sequenced chronologically.

- The children then write an appropriate temporal connective underneath each picture.

Plenary

- Using one child's work, explain that they have created a plan for writing a recount of their visit. Draw attention to the fact that their plan sequences the events as they occurred and includes key words that signal chronology.

- Explain that these are two key features of recount writing and enter them into a class checklist (see Resource Page D for ideas).

Setting the Scene

Objective

We will write a scene-setting opening using description and the past tense

You need: Resource Pages B and C; sequenced photographs of the visit; the children's plans from the previous lesson.

Whole class work

- Referring to the sequenced photographs taken on the visit, explain to the class that today's lesson will focus on writing the opening for their recount.

- Read together the initial paragraph of Resource Page B. In pairs, ask the children to identify which features they feel contribute to a successful opening. Use Resource Page C as a guide.

- Explain that recounts should be written in the past tense.

- In pairs, the children ask their partner to recount something they did yesterday. Using these examples, reinforce what is meant by 'past tense'. List the words the children use to describe what they did, for example:

> walk*ed*, play*ed*, work*ed*, visit*ed*

  Draw attention to the use of '-ed' to indicate the past tense, then locate examples in the first paragraph of the sample text.

- Invite the children to consider why specific details are used, for example, names of people, descriptions of objects/places. ***Details help bring the events to life for the reader, because as they weren't there, they won't know what it was like. It's like drawing a picture with words.***

- Add the features identified to the class checklist. In pairs, the children orally rehearse an opening for their recount incorporating details, the use of the past tense and the use of a temporal connective.

- Select a clear example, and demonstrate how to write an opening. As you scribe the children's suggestions, challenge them to justify their word choice. Refer back to the checklist to ensure all key features have been incorporated.

Independent, pair or guided work

- Using the class checklist and plans created in the previous lesson, the children write a scene-setting opening using the past tense and description/detail.

Plenary

- Referring to the class checklist, encourage several children to share their openings.

- Evaluate using a response sandwich: one good comment, followed by an idea on how to improve the work, followed by a second good comment.

- Identifying one sentence for improvement, demonstrate how to substitute words within the sentence to give the reader a clearer image.

124

Amusing Events and Conclusion

Objective

We will recount a visit using chronological order and ending with a closing statement

You need: Resource Pages B, C and E; whiteboards (one each).

Whole class work

- Revisiting Resource Page B, encourage the children to join in as much as possible as you read the recount through to the end.

- Encourage the children to identify all the key features associated with writing a recount (Resource Page C). Add any additional features identified to the checklist created in the last lesson.

- ***Today's lesson will focus on completing the recount you began yesterday***. Use one child's writing plan to reinforce the importance of continuing to recount events in chronological order and to link events using temporal connectives.

- Reread the fourth paragraph of the example recount which details an amusing event. Prompt the children to deduce why such events are often incorporated into recounts. Answer: to amuse and entertain the reader.

- Reflecting on their own visit, encourage the children to identify a particular event that would amuse or interest a reader. The children scribe their ideas on to whiteboards, then swap with a partner. Allowing the children time to read through the event described, encourage them to identify any errors or elements that could be improved. Feed back any suggestions. These whiteboards can be used during the independent activity to support the children as they write.

- Returning to Resource Page B, focus on the way the ending comments on, or sums up, the events of the day.

- Working in mixed ability pairs, prompt the children to orally rehearse, then share a closing statement for their recount.

Independent, pair or guided work

- Continuing with the work begun in the previous lesson, the children complete their recount, ensuring that events are in chronological order and are linked using temporal connectives.

- Display the checklist as well as the supported composition on amusing events written and refined on their whiteboards during the shared session.

Plenary

- Using the marking ladder (Resource Page E), encourage the children to share and then evaluate their completed recount, identifying elements of success as well as areas for improvement.

- Evaluate using a response sandwich: one good comment, followed by an idea on how to improve the work, followed by a second good comment.

- If possible, give the children a real reason for writing by inviting an audience into the classroom to share their completed recounts.

125

Pupil copymaster

The question hand

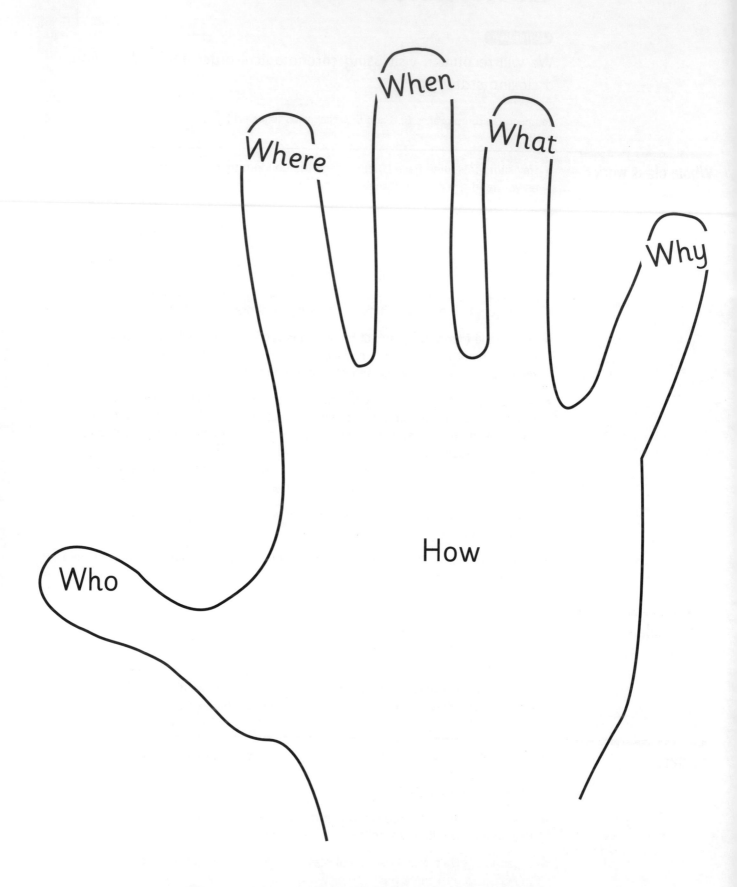

Classworks Literacy Year 1 © Louise Gilbert, Nelson Thornes Ltd 2003

Our visit to the Police Station

Last Monday our class visited the local Police Station. When we got there PC James met us outside and took us through a set of big blue doors into the Reception. He explained that there were twenty policemen and women working at the station.

First he took us to a room full of computers and telephones. He told us that if we rang the police, this is where our call would be answered. He also explained that if we rang we would be asked to give our name and address so we should practise remembering these at home.

Next we went outside to see the police horses. We helped feed a big black one called Molly. She helps the police to control big crowds of people.

Then we visited the cells where they keep people locked up. We all laughed when PC James pretended to lock my friend Tim in there!

Finally PC James told us about all the different ways the police help us before we waved goodbye.

When we got back to school we were all very tired. It had been a very interesting day. I think I would like to be a policeman when I grow up.

Classworks Literacy Year 1 © Louise Gilbert, Nelson Thornes Ltd 2003

(Exemplar analysis)

Example of analysis of our visit to the Police Station

Written in the past tense.

Orientation – scene setting and opening.

Written in chronological order with connectives that signal time.

End by commenting on events.

Use specific names.

Details are vital to bring alive the incidents.

Pick out incidents that are amusing.

Last Monday our class visited the local Police Station. When we got there PC James met us outside and took us through a set of big blue doors into the Reception. He explained that there were twenty policemen and women working at the station.

First he took us to a room full of computers and telephones. He told us that if we rang the police, this is where our call would be answered. He also explained that if we rang we would be asked to give our name and address so we should practise remembering these at home.

Next we went outside to see the police horses. We helped feed a big black one called Molly. She helps the police to control big crowds of people.

Then we visited the cells where they keep people locked up. We all laughed when PC James pretended to lock my friend Tim in there!

Finally PC James told us about all the different ways the police help us before we waved goodbye.

When we got back to school we were all very tired. It had been a very interesting day. I think I would like to be a policeman when I grow up.

(Exemplar material)

Checklists for a recount of a class visit

Example of a checklist for writing questions

- Use a question word at the beginning such as 'who', 'where', 'when', 'what', 'why' or 'how'

- Use a question mark '?' at the end of the sentence rather than a full stop

- The writing must make sense

- The first letter in the sentence must be a capital letter

Example of a checklist for writing a recount

- Write in chronological order

- Use temporal connectives, for example, 'first/ly', 'then', 'next', 'after', 'finally', 'lastly'

- Opening must set the scene

- Include details to bring the events alive for the reader

- Use the past tense

- Recount incidents of interest/ amusement

- Write as if you are 'telling a story' of what happened

- End by commenting on events

(Marking ladder)

Name: _____

Pupil	Objective	Teacher
	My recount contains a scene-setting opening.	
	I recounted events in chronological order.	
	I used temporal connectives.	
	I used the past tense.	
	I used details to bring incidents alive.	
	I used specific names of people, places, objects and so on.	
	I recounted incidents of interest/amusement.	
	I wrote as if I was 'telling a story' of what happened.	
	I ended with comments on events.	
	What could I do to improve my recount next time?	

Poems on a Theme: Food

Outcome

Poems about food written in the style of poems studied

Objectives

Sentence

1 to expect reading to make sense and check if it does not.

3 to read familiar texts aloud with pace and expression appropriate to the grammar, e.g. pausing at the full stops, raising voice for questions.

5 [be taught] other common uses for capitalisation, e.g. for personal titles ('Mr', 'Miss'), headings, book titles, emphasis.

Text

1 to reinforce and apply their word-level skills through shared and guided reading.

2 to use phonological, contextual, grammatical and graphic knowledge to work out, predict and check the meanings of unfamiliar words and to make sense of what they read.

9 to read a variety of poems on similar themes, e.g. families, school, food.

10 to compare and contrast preferences and common themes in stories and poems.

12 through shared and guided writing to apply phonological, graphic knowledge and sight vocabulary to spell words accurately.

15 to use poems or parts of poems as models for own writing, e.g. by substituting words or elaborating on the text.

16 to compose own poetic sentences, using repetitive patterns, carefully selected sentences and imagery.

Planning frame

● Read poems with different themes, identifying poetic techniques.

● Use poems as a planning frame for writing own poems.

How you could plan this unit

Day 1	Day 2	Day 3	Day 4	Day 5
Reading and writing	Reading and writing	Reading and writing	Reading and writing	Reading and writing Critical evaluation of poems. Redraft one of the poems written during the unit using ICT. Use marking ladder
Brainstorming Adjectives	*Alphabet Poems*	*Using Onomatopoeia*	*Recipe Poems*	

Day 6	Day 7
Reading Rehearsing and performing poems aloud with pace and expression	Reading Performing poems to an audience. Creating a class anthology

Brainstorming Adjectives

Objective

We will use appropriate adjectives to create a simple shape poem in the style of one we have read

You need: Resource Pages A–C; a banana.

Whole class work

- Explain to your class that they will be looking at poems about food.

- Without showing them the poem or allowing them to see the title, read through *The Apple* (Resource Page A). ***Can you guess what type of food the poet is describing?***

- Display *The Apple* and discuss the way in which the words have been arranged. Explain that poets may choose to write 'shape poems' because they are eye-catching and interesting to read.

- Reread the poem together. Ask the children to identify what type of words the poem is made from. If necessary remind them of the term 'adjective'.

- Next, focus on how the adjectives have been arranged to create the poem: two adjectives ending with y, followed by an adjective ending in a different phoneme, then the word 'and', then another adjective ending in y.

> Munchy, crunchy, red and juicy

- Show the children a banana, then brainstorm all the words associated with it. Write the words ending with y on one side of the flip chart and words ending with all other letters on the other side.

- Using *The Apple* as a model for writing, demonstrate how to arrange the adjectives the children have brainstormed to create a poem (Resource Page B).

- Demonstrate how to arrange the poem in the shape of a banana.

Independent, pair or guided work

- Using the planning frame (Resource Page C), the children select an item of food then brainstorm all the adjectives associated with it, separating the words into those ending with y and those ending with alternative letters.

- The children arrange their selected adjectives in the planning frame to create a poem.

- Finally, the children draw a clear picture of their item of food in pencil, arrange their poem around this outline, then simply rub away the original pencil lines.

Plenary

- Without sharing the title initially, selected children read their shape poem. The remainder of the class try to guess the item of food being described. The poet can then show their shape poem to reveal the correct answer.

Alphabet Poems

Objective

We will use alliteration to create an alphabet poem

You need: Resource Page D; dictionaries.

Whole class work

- Read *I Like* (Resource Page D). Allow the children time to discuss the poem and its stylistic features in general terms. Can they identify the use of alliteration?

> sizzling sausages ... bubbling beans

Explain what is meant by 'alliteration'.

- Ask the children to continue reading the poem independently, identifying further use of alliteration.

- On a flip chart draw a picture of a lollipop. Encourage the children to brainstorm all the appropriate adjectives beginning with the same initial letter: 'lovely', 'licky' and so on. *How long can you make your alliterative sentence?*

- Introduce the term 'alphabet poem', and recite the alphabet in order. Explain that today's lesson will focus on writing a class alliterative alphabet poem.

- Beginning with the letter 'a', demonstrate how to select an item of food and an appropriate adjective, for example:

> appetising apple

- Suggesting the use of 'banana' for b, prompt the children to brainstorm alliterative adjectives:

> big ... beautiful ... bruised

- Explain that by brainstorming ideas first they can then select the most appropriate adjective to accompany the item of food.

> appetising apples... bruised bananas ... crunchy crisps ... delicious dates ...
> extraordinary eggs ... fantastic fish ...

- Working as a class, continue writing the first five or six lines of the poem, until the children are comfortable with the format.

- Reading through the poem created, encourage the children to suggest a suitable title.

Independent, pair or guided work

- Divide your class into five ability groups. Give each group five consecutive letters of the alphabet, with group 5 taking the additional letters 'y' and 'z'.

- Group 1 should consist of the least able pupils who can draw on the ideas discussed during the whole class session. Group 5 should consist of the most able children.

- Using the format explored during the shared session, the group selects an item of food then brainstorms an accompanying adjective for each letter to create the lines of the poem. Some children may wish to use dictionaries.

Plenary

- Beginning with group 1, encourage one child from each group to read their part of the poem thus creating a completed alphabet poem running from 'a' to 'z'.

133

Using Onomatopoeia

Objectives

We will learn what is meant by the term 'onomatopoeia' and will use it to create a simple poem. We will also learn that capitalisation can be used for emphasis

You need: Resource Pages E and F; whiteboards and pens (one between two).

Whole class work

- Begin by reading *Noisy Food* (Resource Page E). Invite the children to consider what types of word have been chosen to describe the different items of food and the way they are being consumed. Steer thinking towards the use of words that describe sound.

- Introduce the term 'onomatopoeia'. Focusing closely on the shared text, identify the onomatopoeic words:

> munch ... crunch ... crack ... pop ... squelch

  As each word is identified, reinforce the fact that the onomatopoeic word itself sounds like the sound it describes.

- Brainstorm other onomatopoeic words the children can recall, for example:

> hiss ... splash ... stamp ... bang ... crash

  Enjoy exaggerating the sounds as you say the words.

- In pairs, the children read *Sounds Good* (Resource Page F), noting the onomatopoeic words on their whiteboards. Allow each pair time to feed back their collection of words, then prompt the children to consider why a poet may use onomatopoeia when writing.

- Draw attention towards the poem's final line: 'I'M HUNGRY!' Encourage them to identify the fact that capitalisation has been used as a tool by the poet for emphasis.

- Demonstrate how a simple poem can be created using onomatopoeia and capitalisation for effect:

> WHAT A NOISE!
>
> Squelchy jelly,
> Squishy berries,
> Slurpy milkshake,
> Crunchy toast,
> Sizzling chips.
> DELICIOUS!

Independent, pair or guided work

- The children create a simple onomatopoeic poem entitled *What a Noise!* in the same format as the example.

Plenary

- Invite selected children to share their poems. Selecting a strong example for a second reading, encourage the rest of your class to identify the use of onomatopoeia, then add appropriate sound effects to the poem.

Recipe Poems

Objective

We will create a recipe poem using a range of stylistic features

You need: Resource Pages G–I.

Whole class work

- Begin by reading through a selection of the poems written over the previous three days. Invite the children to identify the stylistic features used by the poets and collate the ideas into a checklist (see Resource Page I for ideas).

- Read through *Dragon Feast* (Resource Page G). Allowing the children time to reflect, discuss their general responses to the poem, then ask: *How is the poem written?* Answer: in the style of a recipe. Focus on the way in which the food reflects the dragon's personality and characteristics.

- Encourage the children to identify the stylistic features the poet draws upon. Add any additional features identified to the checklist (for example, rhyme).

- Draw attention to the use of punctuation. Encourage the children to identify the use of a capital letter at the beginning of each line and the positioning of commas and full stops.

- Returning to the idea that the poem is written as a recipe, begin to investigate what types of word the poet has used to convey this idea. Create a list of useful recipe words:

  > a pinch, a portion, mix, add, combine, a handful.

- Encourage the children to suggest an alternative 'character' to write a recipe for: a sea monster, a giant, a fairy/princess, Santa, and so on.

- Brainstorm items of food appropriate to this character, then investigate how these ideas may be developed to incorporate adjectives, alliteration and onomatopoeia (see Resource Page H for ideas).

- Using a combination of demonstration and scribing, create a recipe poem for the chosen character.

Independent, pair or guided work

- Using the first four lines of your modelled poem, invite the children to substitute a character of their choice in place of Santa. They should then brainstorm items of food relevant to that character, and use adjectives, alliteration and onomatopoeia to create a recipe poem.

Plenary

- Encourage the children to share their poems. *Can you guess who the poem is about without hearing the title? What clues did you find in the poem to help you guess?*

- Invite the rest of your class to identify the stylistic features incorporated. Discuss how the use of these features adds to the poem.

The Apple

Munchy, crunchy, red and juicy, scrummy, yummy, smooth and fruity, healthy, shapely round and tasty.

(Pupil copymaster)

The Banana

squashy

scrummy

spotty

squidgy

sunny

peely

tasty

mushy

squishy

bright

soft

smooth

The Banana

Squashy, scrummy, bright and spotty.

Squidgy, sunny, soft and peely.

Tasty, mushy, smooth and squishy.

(Pupil copymaster)

Planning frame

Adjectives ending in other phonemes:

> The food I have chosen is:

Adjectives ending in <u>y</u>

The --------------------

------------------y, -------------------y, ------------------ and ------------------y.

------------------y, -------------------y, ------------------ and ------------------y.

------------------y, -------------------y, ------------------ and ------------------y.

Now turn over the page. Draw a picture of your item of food. Arrange the words of your poem around it.

(**Pupil copymaster**)

I Like

I like sizzling sausages.
I like bubbling beans.
I like mashed potatoes
With gravy and greens.
I like cold ice-cream.
I like chocolate cakes.
But most of all I like
The jellies my Mum makes

John Foster

(**Pupil copymaster**)

Noisy Food

When you're munching crunchy apples
or you're slurping up your soup,
when you're eating crackly crisps
all on your own or a group,
when you're crunching up your cornflakes
or you're popping bubblegum,
or you're sucking at an orange
with such squelches that your mum
says, "Can't you eat more quietly,
that noise is rather rude!"
It's then that you say, "It's not my fault.
I'm eating noisy food."

Marian Swinger

(Pupil copymaster)

Sounds Good

Sausage sizzles,
crispbreads crack;
hot dogs hiss
and flapjacks snap!
Bacon boils
and fritters fry;
apples squelch
in apple pie.
Baked beans bubble,
gravy grumbles;
popcorn pops,
and stomach rumbles ...
I'M HUNGRY!

Judith Nicholls

(Pupil copymaster)

Dragon Feast

If you want to feed a dragon,
start with something hot,
spicy prawns in vindaloo,
the fiercest that you've got.
They like all kinds of fiery food,
red-hot chillies, pickled limes,
sausages in mustard, peppered crab
with toast burned fourteen times.
Follow this with deep-fried mango
in a flaming brandy sauce,
and some of the very strongest mints
to finish with, of course.

Moira Andrew

(**Pupil copymaster**)

A recipe poem

Items of food for Santa

Roast turkey
Roast potatoes
Peas
Carrots
Chocolate log
Christmas cake
Christmas pudding

Extended ideas

Slices of succulent turkey
Crisp roast potatoes
A portion of peas
Crunchy carrots
Squidgy chocolate log

The Perfect Recipe

If Santa knocks upon your door,
And invites himself to tea,
Make him something he'll really love,
By following this recipe.
Mix together:
A portion of peas,
A handful of crisp roast potatoes,
Three slices of succulent turkey,
Crunchy carrots,
And a squidgy chocolate log.
WHAT A FEAST!

Classworks Literacy Year 1 © Louise Gilbert, Nelson Thornes Ltd 2003

(Exemplar material)

Checklist for poems on a theme

- Use adjectives to add detail

- Use alliteration

- Use onomatopoeia

- Use capitalisation for effect

- Use rhyme

- Writing must make sense

- Use capital letters at the beginning of each line

- Use commas at the end of each line apart from the last line in each verse, which uses a full stop

Classworks Literacy Year 1 © Louise Gilbert, Nelson Thornes Ltd 2003

(**Marking ladder**)

Name: _____

Pupil	Objective	Teacher
	I used adjectives to add detail.	
	I used alliteration.	
	I used onomatopoeia.	
	I used capitalisation for effect.	
	My writing makes sense.	
	I used capital letters at the beginning of each line.	
	I used commas at the end of each line apart from the last line in each verse, where I used a full stop.	
	What could I do to improve my poem next time?	

Poems from a Range of Cultures

Outcome

A variety of poems, rhymes and chants based on those read

Objectives

Sentence

1 to expect reading to make sense and check if it does not, and to read aloud using expression appropriate to the grammar of the text.

3 to predict words from preceding words in sentences and investigate the sorts of words that 'fit', suggesting appropriate alternatives, i.e. that make sense.

Text

2 to use phonological, contextual, grammatical and graphic knowledge to work out, predict and check the meanings of unfamiliar words and to make sense of what they read.

3 to choose and read familiar books with concentration and attention, discuss preferences and give reasons.

11 to learn and recite simple poems and rhymes, with actions, and to reread them from the text.

13 to substitute and extend patterns from reading through language play, e.g. by using same lines and introducing new words, extending rhyming or alliterative patterns, adding further rhyming words, lines.

Planning frame

- Write poems in the style of different poets.

- Extend knowledge by sharing experiences of different winter festivals through poetry.

How you could plan this unit

Day 1	Day 2	Day 3	Day 4	Day 5
Talk for writing Identifying and sharing poems, rhymes and chants from around the world	**Reading and writing**	**Reading and writing**	**Reading and writing**	**Reading and writing**
	Alternative Versions	*Action Rhymes*	*An Indian Chant*	*Winter Festivals*

146

Alternative Versions

Objectives

We will recite simple rhymes and reread them from the text. We will suggest alternative words, ones that make sense

You need: Resource Pages A and B; flip chart/whiteboard.

Whole class work

- Begin by humming a traditional nursery rhyme and inviting the children to identify it as quickly as possible. Nominate a child to take the role of the adult – humming the tune of another nursery rhyme for the rest of the class to identify. As the game progresses, scribe the titles of the different rhymes on to a flip chart.

- Looking at the titles, ask the children to recall the collective name for such rhymes. Answer: traditional nursery rhymes.

- Read *Humpty Dumpty* (Resource Page A) together. Ask the children whether any of them have heard of an alternative version of *Humpty Dumpty*.

- ***Today you will write your own alternative version of a well-known rhyme.*** Looking closely at *Humpty Dumpty*, begin to examine the types of word that have been used: names, objects (nouns), action words/doing words (verbs).

- Clarify the fact that when substituting words it is important that the same 'type' of word is chosen to ensure that the rhyme still makes sense.

- Review what is meant by 'rhyme': words that have the same last phonemes, but a different first (and second) phoneme. Using *Humpty Dumpty*, demonstrate how rhyming words can be changed by crossing them out and inserting an alternative:

> ~~ball~~ fall   ~~hens~~ again

As you work, explain your choices in terms of words selected for substitution.

Independent, pair or guided work

- Using Resource Page B, the children substitute words from the original version of *Hickory Dickory Dock* to create an alternative version, as modelled during the shared session.

Plenary

- Invite several children to share their work. Discuss which words they have selected to substitute. ***Have they chosen appropriate alternative words?***

- As a class, recite a variety of the 'alternative rhymes'.

- End the session by reading an alternative version of *Little Miss Muffet*. Reinforce the fact that 'playing with' or substituting words can produce amusing results.

> Little Miss Muffett
> Sat on a tuffet,
> Eating some Irish Stew
> Along came a spider
> Who sat down beside her
> And so she ate him up too.

Action Rhymes

Objective

We will recite simple action rhymes and write an action rhyme of our own

You need: Resource Pages C and D; Post-it™ note.

Whole class work

- *What is an action rhyme?* Perform some well-known examples, for example, *Ten Green Bottles*, *Once I Caught a Fish Alive*. Some children may be more familiar with examples from pop music than these traditional rhymes – use their knowledge as an alternative demonstration (but ask for a preview *before* the lesson...).

- Explain that action rhymes are popular with children from a variety of cultures.

- Introduce *Everything You Do* (Resource Page C), obscuring the final lines 'for I am your shadow!' with a Post-it™ note. Encourage the children to listen carefully to the rhyme, then ask them to consider who they think the 'second voice' belongs to. Once ideas have been collated, remove the Post-it™ note to reveal the answer.

- Recite the rhyme together, adding appropriate actions.

- Weather permitting, take the children outside into the playground to reinforce what is meant by the term 'shadow'. With partners, one child makes movements and the other acts as their shadow. (Some children may get confused and try to 'mirror' the movements – so it is easier to demonstrate this activity in a sunny environment or with a strong spotlight.) You could also repeat this at different times of the day to see how the shadow changes proportions depending on the position of the sun.

- Returning to *Everything You Do*, allow the children time to examine how this simple rhyme has been created. Then, using an enlarged copy of Resource Page D as a writing frame, begin to create a new version, inviting your class to suggest suitable movements.

- Through shared writing, extend the children's knowledge by asking them to justify word choices. Model strategies such as rereading to check for sense.

Independent, pair or guided work

- Using Resource Page D to assist with structure, prompt the children to enter alternative words into the frame to create an alternative action rhyme.

Plenary

- Split the class into two groups, facing each other. Perform a class recital of *Everything You Do*, with one group taking on the role of 'first voice' and the other group the voice of the shadow ('second voice').

- Repeat using an action rhyme written by one of the children during independent work.

An Indian Chant

Objective

We will substitute lines in an Indian chant

You need: Resource Pages E, F and H; a globe or world map; Indian music or photographs of India; whiteboards and pens (one between two).

Whole class work

- Brainstorm some traditional nursery rhymes from British culture and explain that today's lesson will focus on a children's rhythmic chant from India.

- Use the globe or world map to locate the country and, if possible, invite a parent with knowledge of the Indian culture to share a little of their experience with the class. Alternatively, source some photographs and some traditional Indian music.

- Read through *Rani Sits Beside Her Door* (Resource Page E).

- Assist the children in identifying the key features. Ensure the following points are noted and used to compile a checklist (see Resource Page H for ideas):

> The chant is a number rhyme.
>
> The title is the same as the second line.
>
> Each pair of lines rhymes (note the near rhyme in the case of lines 5 and 6).
>
> Commas are used at the end of each line apart from the final line which takes a full stop.

- Explain that in order to create a new version of the chant they are going to substitute every other line (lines 2, 4 and 6).

- Reread the first two lines, identifying the two rhyming words ('four' and 'door'). Explain that the whole of the second line must be substituted and invite the children to create an alternative second line, for example:

> Rani sits on the floor.

Point out that the second line is also the title.

- Reread lines 3 and 4. Ask the children to scribe on whiteboards their ideas for an alternative fourth line.

Independent, pair or guided work

- Using Resource Page F as a writing frame and the class checklist, the children create a new version of the chant by writing alternative lines 2, 4 and 6.

Plenary

- Explore the alternative second lines. ***How many different words have we found that rhyme with 'four'?***

- ***Does the length of the second line affect the way the chant is read?***

- ***Which ideas are better and why?***

Winter Festivals

Objective

We will use brainstorming as a tool for gathering ideas, and then write a poem about a cultural festival

You need: Resource Pages G–I.

Whole class work

- Read the poem *Holi, Festival of Colour* (Resource Page G), explaining that Holi is the Hindu festival of Spring (colours, celebrations and flowers).

- Ask what the poem tells us about the way Hindus celebrate this festival.

- Modelling how to use context as a strategy, encourage the children to suggest meanings for the words or phrases that may be unfamiliar to them.

Sweetmeats:	sweets or chocolates
Coloured waters:	Royal courts in North India refined the festival to an art form. Men demonstrated their equestrian skills while riding through water coloured with saffron and an orange-red dye from the kasuda flower.

- Prompt the children to identify a time of celebration they have experienced, for example, their own or a friend's birthday. Referring to the poem, they compare and contrast the ways in which birthdays and Holi are celebrated: meeting with family, dancing and singing, hanging balloons and eating are common to both, whereas coloured water is only used during the festival of Holi.

- Explain that they are going to create a poem about a time of celebration using the structure and key features of the chant analysed in the previous lesson.

- In pairs, the children brainstorm the ways they celebrate their birthdays. Each child reports one way their partner celebrates. Make a list or spidergram of ideas.

- Demonstrate how to refine the ideas collated by striking through ideas you no longer consider suitable, improving word choice and drawing ideas together.

- Together, compile these refined notes into a simple poem (see example 2, Resource Page H). As you work, extend the children's understanding by challenging their contributions as well as exploring strategies for spelling unknown words.

Independent, pair or guided work

- In pairs, the children brainstorm all the ways in which they celebrate a winter festival (Christmas, Diwali, Hanukkah and so on). The children work cooperatively to produce a joint poem based on your model.

Plenary

- Invite some children to share their initial notes (spidergram, list). Encourage them to discuss how they refined their ideas.

- Select several pairs to perform their poems. The rest of your class discuss the similarities and differences between the celebrations.

- Using the marking ladder (Resource Page I), encourage the children to self-evaluate their work, identifying areas of success and areas for improvement.

Humpty Dumpty

Humpty Dumpty sat on a wall,

Humpty Dumpty had a great fall.

All the King's horses

And all the King's men

Couldn't put Humpty together again.

Pupil copymaster

Hickory Dickory Dock

Hickory Dickory Dock,

The mouse ran up the clock.

The clock struck one,

The mouse ran down,

Hickory Dickory Dock,

Tick tock, tick tock.

(Pupil copymaster)

Everything You Do

You shake your head
    I shake mine

You wave your hand
    I wave mine

You stamp your foot
    I stamp mine

You clap your hand
    I clap mine

You touch your nose
    I touch mine

You pull your ear
    I pull mine

You jump in the air
    I jump too

You run on the spot
    I run too

Everything you do
    I do too

And wherever you go

    I go too
     for I am –
      your
       Shadow!

Mabel Segun

Pupil copymaster

Writing frame

You _____ your _____

         I _____ mine

You _____ your _____

         I _____ mine

You _____ your _____

         I _____ mine

You _____ your _____

         I _____ mine

You _____ your _____

         I _____ mine

You _____ your _____

         I _____ mine

Everything you do

         I do too

And wherever you go

         I go too

           for I am –

             your

             Shadow!

Based on Everything You Do, *by Mabel Segun*

(Pupil copymaster)

Rani Sits Beside Her Door

One, two, three, four,

Rani sits beside her door,

Five, six, seven, eight,

Study hard, don't leave it late,

Counting, learning, nine and ten,

Rani calls out Na-ma-stay-friend.

Translation by kind permission of LCP

Classworks Literacy Year 1 © Louise Gilbert, Nelson Thornes Ltd 2003

Writing frame for counting

One, two, three, four,

Five, six, seven, eight,

Counting, learning, nine and ten,

Holi, Festival of Colour

Throw the waters, coloured waters,

Holi Festival's here.

Musicians playing, drummers beating,

Processions leading through the streets.

Joyfully children dance and sing,

Holi the colourful Festival of Spring.

Friends and relations all will meet,

Sweetmeats, balloons, for when they greet.

Throw the waters, coloured waters,

For Holi Festival's here!

Punitha Perinparaja

Checklists for poems from a range of cultures

Example of a checklist for writing a rhythmic chant ①

- Use numbers to create a number rhyme

- Repeat the title as the second line

- Make sure each pair of lines rhymes (or near-rhymes)

- Use a comma at the end of each line apart from the final line, which has a full stop

Example of modelling a simple poem ②

Balloons and Presents on the Floor

One, two, three, four,
Balloons and presents on the floor,
Five, six, seven, eight,
Wobbly jelly and a chocolate cake,
Dancing, singing, nine and ten,
Gather together family and friend.

Marking ladder

Name: _____

Pupil	Objective	Teacher
	I used numbers to create a number rhyme.	
	My title is the same as the second line.	
	Each pair of lines rhymes (or near-rhymes).	
	I used commas at the end of each line apart from the final line, where I used a full stop.	
	My writing makes sense.	
	What could I do to improve my poem next time?	

Poems with a Pattern

Outcome

Poetic sentences using repetitive patterns; performance of our own poems and listening to those of others

Objectives

Sentence

1 to expect reading to make sense and check if it does not.

3 to read familiar texts aloud with pace and expression appropriate to the grammar, e.g. pausing at full stops, raising voice for questions.

6 through reading and writing, to reinforce knowledge of term 'sentence' from previous terms.

7 to add question marks to questions.

Text

1 to reinforce and apply their word-level skills through shared and guided reading.

2 use phonological, contextual, grammatical and graphic knowledge to work out, predict and check the meanings of unfamiliar words and to make sense of what they read.

4 to read with sufficient concentration to complete a text, and to identify preferences and give reasons.

11 to collect class and individual favourite poems for class anthologies, participate in reading aloud.

12 through shared and guided writing to apply phonological, graphic knowledge and sight vocabulary to spell words accurately.

16 to compose own poetic sentences, using repetitive patterns, carefully selected sentences and imagery.

Planning frame

- Read a range of poems that have strong imagery and use patterned and predictable structures.

- Use these structures as a basis for own writing.

How you could plan this unit

Day 1	Day 2	Day 3	Day 4	Day 5
Talk for writing Read a selection of poems with pace and expression, identifying use of imagery	**Talk for writing and writing**	**Writing**	**Reading** Identifying onomatopoeia, alliteration and rhyme scheme in *The Sound Collector* (Resource Page B)	**Writing**
	Descriptive Language	*Powerful Imagery*		*A Sense Poem*

Day 6	Day 7	Day 8	Day 9	Day 10
Writing Writing an alternative version of *The Sound Collector* using an alternative sense: taste, sight, touch or smell	**Writing** Using questions in poetry. Creating a humorous poem entitled *Why?* 'Why did you put a spider down my back?' 'Why did you put worms in my bed?' and so on	**Reading and writing**	**Reading and writing** Group and self-evaluation of own poems. Collecting favourite poems to create a class anthology	**Performance** Performance of poems
		Using Personification		

Descriptive Language

Objective

We will begin to use descriptive language

You need: Resource Page A; flip chart/whiteboard; picture of an animal.

Whole class work

- Describe the physical features of a member of your class. Encourage the children to suggest who you could be describing. Invite these children to stand up and encourage the rest of the class to identify the additional information that would assist in identifying the chosen child: <u>curly</u> hair, <u>blue</u> glasses, brown eyes, girl/boy.

> I'm thinking of a child with brown hair who wears glasses.

- In pairs, the children describe the physical features of their friend in as much depth as possible.

- Explain that the use of descriptive language is an important tool used by poets to create 'imagery' – detailed pictures in the head of the reader.

- Draw a simple picture of a ladybird in the middle of the flip chart. Brainstorm a variety of words that could be used to describe the ladybird's appearance. List words that describe what the ladybird could be doing: 'sleeping', 'eating' and so on (see Resource Page A).

- Discuss which words are powerful in creating an image: 'scarlet' as opposed to 'red', 'crawling' as opposed to 'walking'. Demonstrate how these ideas can be used to write a poem (Resource Page A).

- Hold up a picture of another animal. Dividing the class in two, encourage the children in one half to brainstorm words that describe the animal's appearance, while the other half select words that describe what the animal could be doing.

- Select an idea from each half of the class and demonstrate how to combine the two describing words into a poetic sentence, for example:

> A stripy tiger prowling.

Independent, pair or guided work

- The children choose their own animal and brainstorm words to describe the physical characteristics and what the animal might be doing. The children combine the ideas into poetic sentences as modelled during the shared session.

Plenary

- Ask the children to pass their poetic sentences to a partner. The partner should then select the sentence they feel conveys the most powerful image.

- Share these selected sentences with the class for analysis. Consider use of interesting describing words, powerful verbs, alliteration and onomatopoeia.

Powerful Imagery

Objective

We will write imaginative poetic sentences, selecting words carefully to create powerful imagery

You need: Resource Page F; a cloudy day! – or photographs of clouds in the sky; whiteboards and pens.

Whole class work

- Take the children outside. If weather permits, encourage them to lie on their backs, or simply look up towards the sky. Allow time to look at the clouds passing. *Can you see any pictures in the clouds? (Faces, animals, objects?)*

- Return to the classroom and allow the children time to recall and discuss the images they have seen, firstly with a partner, then with the whole class.

- *Can you refine your ideas in order to create more powerful imagery? How could we add to that description? Can you think of a more powerful word?*

- Explain that you saw an image of a dragon in the clouds. Invite the children to close their eyes and imagine what this dragon may have looked like.

- Once they have a clear picture in their heads, encourage them to scribe the word 'dragon' in the middle of their whiteboards. Now ask them to add some words to describe its appearance:

> A scaly dragon.

- The children swap boards with a partner. The partner reads the sentence then strengthens the description by adding more details:

> A scaly dragon with claws as sharp as knives.

- Finally the board is passed back to the original child who rereads the sentence, checks for capital letters and full stops, and selects one word to exchange (or add) for a more powerful image:

> A snarling dragon with claws as sharp as knives.

- Share and analyse the finished sentences identifying use (intentional or otherwise) of onomatopoeia, alliteration or simile, then create a class checklist for writing poetic sentences (see Resource Page F for ideas).

Independent, pair or guided work

- Using the class checklist, the children write poetic sentences to describe the images they saw in the clouds.

Plenary

- Encourage the children to identify and then share their most powerful sentence. As they read, encourage the rest of the class to close their eyes and listen to the words used. *Can you recreate the image in your head?*

- Selecting one sentence, invite the children to assist you in strengthening the imagery through careful word choice.

A Sense Poem

Objective

We will use onomatopoeia, alliteration and rhyme to write a poem based on *The Sound Collector,* using sounds from school

You need: Resource Pages B–D and F.

Whole class work

- Reread *The Sound Collector* (Resource Page B). Encourage the children to recall the key features/stylistic devices the poem incorporates (Resource Page C).

- Explain that today's lesson will focus on creating an alternative version of this poem, retaining these key features. Use the children's suggestions to create a class checklist to support their rewriting (see Resource Page F for ideas).

- *What sounds would the collector remove if he visited school?*

- Take a 'sound walk' in and around the building – canteen, playground, office, other classrooms – listening to the range of sounds.

- Returning to the classroom, gather the different sounds into a list.

- Ask one child secretly to select one of the sounds from the list, for example the computer humming. Invite them to recreate that sound using their voice, then encourage the rest of the class to identify the source of the sound impersonated.

- Show the planning frame (Resource Page D). Explain that their alternative version of the poem will concern the sound collector's visit to a school as opposed to his visit to a house, as in the original version.

- Using the list of sounds identified during the walk, demonstrate how to complete the first few lines of the poem:

> The humming of the computer
> The scraping of the chairs...

Independent, pair or guided work

- Using Resource Page D and the class checklist, the children rewrite the middle section of *The Sound Collector,* substituting sounds from around the home for those associated with school.

- Higher attaining children should incorporate the rhyme scheme from the original poem as well as onomatopoeia and alliteration.

Plenary

- Encourage several children to share their alternative versions of the poem.

- Referring to the checklist, evaluate using a response sandwich: one good comment – one idea for improvement – another good comment.

- Make explicit any use of rhyme, alliteration and onomatopoeia. Discuss how these features enhance the poem.

Using Personification

Objective

We will learn what is meant by the term 'personification', and use personification to write poetic sentences

You need: Resource Page E; flip chart; whiteboards and pens (one between two).

Whole class work

- Read *The Clown's Last Joke* (Resource Page E).

- In pairs, the children discuss and then share features of the poem/points of interest they have identified:
  - the use of a question mark
  - the repetitive pattern in the middle section of the text incorporating positional language (in, under, inside, between)
  - use of the words 'nose' and 'knows' at the end of the last two lines
  - the image produced by the use of the line 'In a bundle of tricks'.

- Draw attention to the line 'Inside a grinning shoe'. Ask them to consider what effect the poet wanted to create by using this combination of words. *Have you ever seen a grinning shoe? What would you normally associate 'grinning' with?*

- Explain that poets sometimes use personification as a tool to make a poem more attention-grabbing. This means giving objects, like shoes, human characteristics.

- Define what is meant by 'human characteristics' and then create a list of examples:

> smiling, dancing, laughing, winking, shivering, grabbing, whispering.

Encourage the children to suggest additions to the list once confident.

- Explain that they are going to create a simple poem entitled *One Day* using short sentences that incorporate personification.

- Brainstorm what sort of person the poem could be about: a dancer, a police officer, a cook and so on.

- Scribe the title on to a flip chart and demonstrate how to rehearse the initial sentences orally before writing:

> The waves danced   The stars winked   And the wind whispered.

- Using a whiteboard and the list of human characteristics, the children work in pairs to create the next line. Allow time to share and discuss ideas.

Independent, pair or guided work

- The children complete their poem *One Day* by writing short poetic sentences that incorporate personification.

Plenary

- Reinforce the fact that poets select unusual or surprising word combinations to intrigue their audience.

- Invite the children to share their completed poems or favourite lines of personification.

- Discuss the way in which personification also acts as a tool to strengthen imagery.

(Pupil copymaster)

The Ladybird

scarlet
spotty
red
delicate
beautiful
dainty
tiny

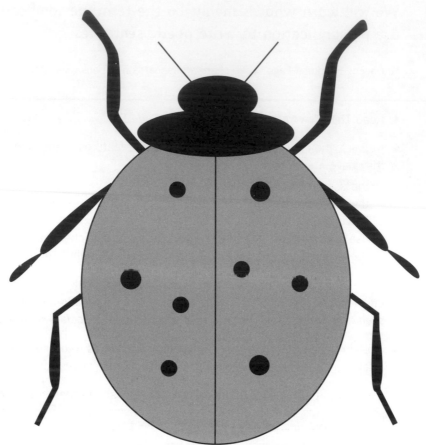

crawling
creeping
flying
dancing
munching
hiding
sleeping

THE LADYBIRD

A scarlet ladybird crawling,
A spotty ladybird creeping,
A red ladybird flying,
A delicate ladybird dancing,
A beautiful ladybird munching,
A dainty ladybird hiding,
A tiny ladybird sleeping.

Pupil copymaster

The Sound Collector

A stranger called this morning
Dressed all in black and grey
Put every sound into a bag
And carried them away.

The whistling of the kettle
The turning of the lock
The purring of the kitten
The ticking of the clock
The popping of the toaster
The crunching of the flakes
When you spread the marmalade
The scraping noise it makes
The hissing of the frying pan
The ticking of the grill
The bubbling of the bathtub
As it starts to fill
The drumming of the raindrops
On the window pane
When you do the washing up
The gurgle of the drain
The crying of the baby
The squeaking of the chair
The swishing of the curtain
The creaking of the stair

A stranger called this morning
He didn't leave his name
He left us only silence
Life will never be the same.

Roger McGough

(Exemplar analysis)

Example of analysis of *The Sound Collector*

A stranger called this morning
Dressed all in black and grey
Put every sound into a bag
And carried them away.

The whistling of the kettle
The turning of the lock
The purring of the kitten
The ticking of the clock
The popping of the toaster
The crunching of the flakes
When you spread the marmalade
The scraping noise it makes

The hissing of the frying pan
The ticking of the grill
The bubbling of the bathtub
As it starts to fill
The drumming of the raindrops
On the window pane
When you do the washing up
The gurgle of the drain
The crying of the baby
The squeaking of the chair
The swishing of the curtain
The creaking of the stair

A stranger called this morning
He didn't leave his name
He left us only silence
Life will never be the same.

Roger McGough

Use of onomatopoeia.

Use of alliteration.

Capital letters at the beginning of every line.

Rhyme scheme.

Many lines follow same format, 'The ... of the ...'.

No use of full stops or commas in this section of the poem.

(Pupil copymaster)

The Sound Collector writing frame

A stranger called at school this morning
Dressed all in black and grey
Put every sound into a bag
And carried them away.

_____

_____

_____

_____

_____

_____

A stranger called at school this morning
He didn't leave his name
He left us only silence
Life will never be the same.

based on The Sound Collector *by Roger McGough*

The Clown's Last Joke

Whatever became of the clown's red nose?
They found a farewell note
In a bundle of tricks.

They found a shaggy eyebrow
Under a floppy hat.

They found a painted cheek
Inside a grinning shoe.

They found a rubber ball
Between baggy trousers.

But they never found the clown's red nose.

They pulled out all the drawers
They turned over sheets
But whatever became of the clown's red nose?
Only God in heaven knows.

John Agard

Classworks Literacy Year 1 © Louise Gilbert, Nelson Thornes Ltd 2003

(Exemplar material)

Checklists for poems with a pattern

Example of a checklist for writing a poetic sentence

- Start with your key word: *dolphin*

- Add words to describe its appearance/what it is like: *a graceful dolphin*

- Add words to describe what it is doing (if appropriate): *a graceful dolphin jumping in the ocean*

- Reread your chosen words – can you make some more powerful? *a graceful dolphin leaping in the ocean*

- Ensure that your sentence has a capital letter and a full stop: *A graceful dolphin leaping in the ocean.*

- Ensure that your sentence makes sense

- Reread your sentence – do you want to make any modifications? *A graceful dolphin leaping in the sparkling ocean.*

Example of a checklist for *The Sense Collector*

- Use onomatopoeia: 'pop', 'tick', 'crunch'

- Use alliteration: **bubbling of the bathtub**

- Use rhyme:
  The whistling of the kettle
  The turning of the lock
  The purring of the kitten
  The ticking of the clock

- Use a capital letter at the beginning of each line

- Do not use full stops or commas

Classworks Literacy Year 1 © Louise Gilbert, Nelson Thornes Ltd 2003

(**Marking ladder**)

Name: _____

Pupil	Objective	Teacher
	I have carefully selected words to create strong images.	
	My poem includes onomatopoeia.	
	It includes alliteration.	
	It includes rhyme.	
	It includes personification.	
	I have used a capital letter at the beginning of every line.	
	My writing makes sense.	
	What could I do to improve my poem next time?	

Stories with Familiar Settings

Outcome

A simple recount or story based on a personal experience

Objectives	**Sentence**
	1 to expect written text to make sense and to check for sense if it does not.
	4 to write captions and simple sentences, and to reread, recognising whether or not they make sense, e.g. missing words, wrong word order.
	8 to begin using full stops to demarcate sentences.
	9 to use a capital letter for the personal pronoun 'I' and for the start of a sentence.
	Text
	1 to reinforce and apply their word-level skills through shared and guided reading.
	3 to notice the difference between spoken and written forms through retelling known stories; compare oral versions with the written text.
	5 to describe story settings and incidents and relate them to own experience and that of others.
	8 through shared and guided reading to apply phonological, graphic knowledge and sight vocabulary to spell words accurately.
	9 to write about events in personal experience linked to a variety of familiar incidents from stories.

Planning frame

- Read and discuss a familiar setting.
- Discuss sequencing events from the story.
- Practise writing sequences.
- Write own first-person narrative.

How you could plan this unit

Day 1	Day 2	Day 3	Day 4	Day 5
Talk for writing	Reading	Writing	Writing	Writing Writing the end of a story based on personal experience
First Day at School	*Sequencing Events*	*Writing Sentences*	*Writing in the First Person*	

First Day at School

Objective

We will describe story settings and incidents and relate them to our own experience and that of others

You need: Resource Page A; A4 plain paper.

Whole class work

- Read *Joe's First Day* (Resource Page A) to the children. Encourage the children to discuss their immediate response to the text. Use questions to ensure that all elements of the story are examined:

> When he woke up how did Joe feel about his first day at school?
>
> How do you know?
>
> At what point did Joe become worried?
>
> What words would you use to describe Mrs Jones?

- Prompt the children to identify the range of emotions that Joe experienced throughout the day – excitement, worry, upset, enjoyment. Discuss what triggered these emotions.

- Invite one or two more confident children to recount their first day at school. As they share their experience, encourage them to add as many details as they can as well as specify the range of emotions they felt throughout the day.

- In pairs, the children recount their own personal recollections of their first day at school as modelled above. As one child speaks the other should listen attentively before the roles are reversed.

- Select several children of differing abilities to share their 'first day' experience with the whole class. Encourage the class to identify similarities and differences between each child's experience. ***Was one similar memory shared by everyone?***

Independent, pair or guided work

- Give lower attaining children the opportunity to explore memories of their first day at school through role play, followed by a discussion to encourage them to compare or relate their own experience to that of others.

- Some children could use pictures and words to compare their own experience with that of Joe. On one side of the A4 paper they record experiences or emotions they shared with Joe, whereas on the other side they record personal experiences that differed from those in the story.

Plenary

- Encourage the children to identify which emotions are shared by everyone on their first day of school.

- Invite them to consider how younger children just starting school may be feeling. ***How could you help make this time a more positive experience for them?***

Sequencing Events

Objective

We will sequence the events in a story

You need: Resource Pages A and B; a teddy bear.

Whole class work	• Reread Resource Page A, *Joe's First Day*. Explain that as you read the children should focus on identifying the sequence of events (the order in which things happen in the story).
	• Removing the text from the children's view, encourage your class to recall the main events in sequence. As they recall each event, demonstrate how to record the sequence by drawing simple pictures linked by arrows.
	• Using an enlarged copy of Resource Page B, explain that some of the sentences from the story have been sequenced incorrectly. The children read the sentences with you then identify the order in which they appear in the story. As they re-order the sentences, encourage them to discuss their reasoning and thought processes.
	• The children sit in a circle. Explain that as a class they are going to retell the story of *Joe's First Day*. Using the pictures and arrows drawn earlier, model how to retell the beginning of the story using appropriate language:

> One day Joe leaped out of bed. He was so excited about his first day at school.

• Explain that you are going to pass the story around the circle and each child should continue it by adding the next sentence, for example:

> He ran downstairs for breakfast.

Continue around the circle, encouraging each child to add a sentence until the story is completed.

Independent, pair or guided work	• The children record the sequence of events as they occurred in *Joe's First Day* using pictures linked by arrows.
Plenary	• Invite one child to share their work. ***Have they sequenced the events correctly?***
	• Show the children the teddy bear. Explain that this is 'Percy', Joe's teddy from the story. Assist them in retelling the story from Percy's point of view.

Writing Sentences

Objectives

We will gather ideas for writing. We will learn what a sentence is

You need: Resource Pages C and D; flip chart.

Whole class work

- Explain that having read and sequenced a story about somebody else's first day, this lesson will focus on gathering ideas in preparation for writing their own story.

- Begin by telling your own personal story about a first day – as teacher or pupil. Before you conclude your story, encourage the children to suggest a suitable ending. Emphasise that an ending must follow on logically from the rest of the story.

- Select one child to assist you in demonstrating how to gather ideas and create a simple story plan. *How did you travel to school on your first day? Can you draw a picture on the flip chart to show us?*

- Ask the child to identify one main event that happened at school. Again represent with a picture, and link the pictures with an arrow to indicate the sequence of events.

- Conclude the story plan with a picture to indicate what happened at the end of the school day, adding an arrow leading from the second picture to the third.

- Referring back to the pictures, ask the child how they felt at each point. Represent this with an appropriate face drawn next to each picture: happy, worried and so on.

- Show the children an enlarged copy of Resource Page C and read through the words together. In pairs, the children identify what is wrong with this sentence:
  - It doesn't make sense.
  - There is no capital letter at the beginning.
  - There is no full stop at the end.

- Select one pair of children to re-order the sentence correctly, ensuring it has a capital letter at the beginning, a full stop at the end and that it makes sense. Explain that these three key features should apply to every sentence they write. Enter these points on to the class checklist (see Resource Page D for ideas).

- Select a picture on the flip chart and ask the children to think of an accompanying sentence. Ask one child to scribe their suggested sentence underneath the picture, ensuring that it incorporates the three key features identified above.

Independent, pair or guided work

- The children draw three simple pictures linked by arrows that record:
  - how they came to school
  - one main event that happened during the day
  - something that happened at the end of the school day.
  Ask them to add pictures of faces to indicate how they felt at each point.

- The children add an accompanying sentence to one of the three pictures using the checklist as a support.

Plenary

- Allow several children to share their story plans and their accompanying sentence. As a class, review their use of the three key features of a sentence.

- In pairs, the children plan sentences orally for the remaining two pictures.

Writing in the First Person

Objectives

We will write a story based on personal experience. We will remember to use a capital letter for 'I'

You need: Resource Page D; flip chart; whiteboards and pens (one between two); cassette recorder.

Whole class work

- Explain to your class that over the next two days they are going to write a story entitled *My First Day at School*, based on their own personal experience.

- Explain that they are going to write the story as if they were telling it to somebody else and this will involve using the word 'I'. ***'I' is always written with a capital letter.***

- Reinforce this use of capitalisation by dictating a simple sentence, for example: 'My dog and I like to play.' Invite a child to scribe the sentence on to the flip chart. Encourage your class to recall other key features a sentence must incorporate.

- Select one child's story plan from the previous lesson. Focusing on the first picture, demonstrate how to write the beginning of a simple story (a recount), for example:

  > I went to school by car with my mum. I felt scared.

  Begin to create a checklist for writing a simple story (see Resource Page D for ideas).

- Draw attention to the second picture. Using the demonstrated writing as a model, invite the children to suggest two sentences that would tell the reader what happened at this point in the story and what emotions were being felt, for example:

  > Lucy and I played with the toy cars. I felt happy.

  Scribe this sentence omitting full stops and capitals. The children identify the mistakes.

- Remind the children of the features identified in the checklist. Using whiteboards and pens, the children work in pairs to devise and scribe two sentences for the third picture in the plan. Encourage the children to reread their work before sharing it with the class. Discuss which sentences are more suitable than others and why.

- Encourage the children to brainstorm words they might need for their story: 'school', 'play', 'felt', words to describe emotions. Create a word bank they can refer to.

Independent, pair or guided work

- Using the class checklist and story plans, the children create a simple story (or recount), by writing two sentences for each picture, the first detailing what happened at that point in the story, the second detailing emotions experienced.

- Lower attaining children could discuss ideas with an adult before recording their sentences on tape using a cassette recorder.

Plenary

- The children listen carefully to the recorded story. Prompt them to identify the end of each sentence by raising their hand in the air.

- Select one of the sentences to scribe on to the flip chart. The children advise on punctuation. Reread the sentence together and use the checklist to ascertain that all the key features have been incorporated.

Joe's First Day

Today was a very special day. It was going to be Joe's first day at school. At six o'clock Joe leaped out of bed, carefully put on his new uniform and raced downstairs. He was so excited he nearly spilled his cornflakes all over his clean white shirt. Finally Mum said it was time to leave and Joe stuffed his favourite teddy, Percy, into his rucksack and ran out of the door.

As they approached the school gates Joe looked towards all the bigger children running around the playground. Joe's smile disappeared and he gripped his mum's hand tightly.

Mum led Joe across the playground and into his new classroom. Mrs Jones, his new teacher, met them both with a smile. 'Good morning, Joe,' she said. Joe looked around nervously at all the other new children, then burst into tears.

'Oh, Joe,' said Mum, 'You've been looking forward to starting school for so long!'

Just then Mum spotted Percy sticking out of the top of Joe's rucksack. Gently she pulled him out and handed the scruffy teddy bear to Joe. 'Look,' she said, 'you will soon make new friends but until you get to know the other children, Percy will keep you company'.

After Mum left, Joe stood in a corner of the classroom holding Percy tightly in both hands. He watched quietly as all the other children played with the Lego, cars, sand and water. All of a sudden a little boy handed Joe a spade. 'Do you know how to make sand castles?' he asked. 'Of course,' said Joe, taking the spade, and together they made a palace fit for a king. It was decorated with stones and shells and Mrs Jones thought it was the best she'd ever seen.

Suddenly Mrs Jones clapped her hands and asked all the children to begin tidying away. When Joe asked her why she explained that it was nearly time to go home. 'Time to go home?' said Joe. 'But we've only just arrived!'

'You and Jack have been making that castle all morning,' exclaimed Mrs Jones.

When his mum arrived Joe ran to her beaming from ear to ear. 'I made a friend called Jack.' he said. 'We made a huge castle from sand, and tomorrow we're going to do painting and play with the Lego and …'

'Oh, so you are going to come back tomorrow?' smiled Mum.

'Oh, yes,' said Joe, 'I love going to school. In fact I don't even think I'll need to bring Percy in the morning. He doesn't like getting all painty and I won't have time to feel lonely with all the new friends I've made.'

Classworks Literacy Year 1 © Louise Gilbert, Nelson Thornes Ltd 2003

Story plan

When his mum arrived Joe ran to her beaming from ear to ear.

Joe stood in a corner of the classroom holding Percy tightly in both hands.

Today was a very special day.

Suddenly Mrs Jones clapped her hands and asked all the children to begin tidying away.

Mum led Joe across the playground and into his new classroom.

special was

day. Today a very

(Exemplar material)

Checklists for stories with familiar settings

Example of a checklist for writing a simple sentence

- Use a capital letter at the beginning of a sentence
- Use a full stop at the end of a sentence
- The sentence must make sense

Example of a checklist for writing a story based on personal experience

- Use a capital letter for the word 'I'
- Use a capital letter at the beginning of each sentence
- Use a full stop at the end of each sentence
- The writing must make sense
- Write as if you are telling a story

(**Marking ladder**)

Name: _____

Pupil	Objective	Teacher
	I used a capital letter for the word 'I'.	
	I used a capital letter at the beginning of each sentence.	
	I used a full stop at the end of each sentence.	
	My work makes sense.	
	I wrote as if 'telling a story' of what happened.	
	What could I do to improve my story next time?	

Word-level starter activities

Starter 1

- Using alphabet cards (a–z) place the vowels face down in a small box and the consonants in another. Invite a child to select two cards from the consonant box and one from the box of vowels. Encourage the children to place the vowel in between the two consonants to create a CVC word. The children should then blend the phonemes together to read the word and decide whether it is real or made up.

Starter 2

- Write a CVC word onto the flip chart, for example, 'hen'. Invite a child to change one letter to make a new word, for example, pen, scribing the new word underneath. Investigate how long a string of words can be created then begin again with a new start word.

Starter 3

- Play 'I spy'. Ask a child to secretly select an object in sight then give its initial letter or phoneme as a clue. The rest of the class should then guess the identity of the object. This game can be extended by giving the final or medial phoneme as a clue as opposed to the initial letter.

Starter 4

- Sit the children in a circle. Decide on a starting word, for example, 'cat'. Going around the circle ask each child to add a word that begins with the same initial letter. Extend the activity by going around the circle again with each child adding a word with the same final phoneme or containing the same medial vowel phoneme.

Starter 5

- Recite a well known nursery rhyme with the children then identify the rhyming words it incorporates. Use these words to generate rhyming strings.

Starter 6

- Write a CVC word onto the board, for example, 'hat'. Explain to the children that to create a word that rhymes all they need do is replace the initial letter with another consonant or 'onset'. Investigate how many rhyming words can be generated.

Starter 7

- Revise the spelling of a consonant digraph, for example, <u>ch</u>, <u>ck</u>, <u>ng</u>. Encourage the children to brainstorm a list of words which use it, then create sentences which incorporate some of the words collected.

Starter 8

- Write a CCVC or CVCC word onto a piece of paper, then cut the word up into the individual letters. Jumble the letters, then challenge the children to unscramble them to identify the original word.

Starter 9

- Write a selection of the children's names onto a flip chart. Ask the class to identify any words within the names, for example, <u>Car</u>ol, H<u>ann</u>ah, J<u>ame</u>s.

Starter 10

- Hold up an object or picture of an object. Ask the children to identify the initial/final/medial phoneme, then scribe the appropriate letter/letters onto a whiteboard.

Starter 11

- Place a variety of objects on the floor, most of which begin with the same initial letter but with a few 'red herrings' added. Hold up a card with the initial letter, then ask the children to identify and collect all the objects beginning with this phoneme. This game can easily be adapted to focus on hearing and identifying final or medial sounds.

Starter 12

- Create 'silly sentences' using alliteration. Once given an initial phoneme more able children may be able to work with a partner to create an alliterative sentence whereas less able children could complete a sentence begun by an adult. For example, 'Henry the huge horse hated ...'

Starter 13

- Give each child an object. Ask one child to hold their object in the air. Children with objects beginning with the same initial phoneme should then also hold these up. Each child should say the name of their object.

Starter 14

- Select two letters to focus on during the activity and write these on a flip chart. Hold up an object beginning with one of the letters and ask the children to point to the appropriate one. This activity can be easily adapted to focus on final or medial phonemes.

Starter 15

- Sitting in a circle place four letter cards in the centre, for example, l, m, n, s. Give each child an object beginning with one of these phonemes. Ask the children to place their object next to the appropriate letter.

Starter 16

- Give each child a letter of the alphabet. Call out a word, for example, 'car' and ask the children who have a letter to make this word to come to the front of the class. Once the children have made the word ask the rest of the class to look carefully at the letter they are holding. If they think they can add their letter to the existing word (for example, 't' to create 'cart') or exchange places with an existing letter (for example, 'n' to create 'can') they should come out to the front and create the new word.

Starter 17

- Secretly write a word on the board, then cover it with a strip of card. Reveal the word one letter at a time asking the children to guess the final word.

Starter 18

- Write the beginning of a word on the board, for example, 'tra'. Invite the children to list on their whiteboards as many words as they can think of beginning with these letters.

Starter 19

- Hold up an object or picture of an object, such as a doll. Explain to the children that you are going to write the word on the board. Spell the word incorrectly, for example, 'boll', 'don', 'dall', then invite the children to identify which part of the word has been incorrectly represented before making appropriate changes.

Starter 20

- Give each pair of children a whiteboard. Call out words appropriate to the ability of the group, then ask the children to write the word on their board.

Starter 21

- Play phoneme or high frequency word bingo. Make bingo cards, each with about nine phonemes or high frequency words on. Give each child a 'bingo card'. Slowly read out the phonemes/words allowing time for the children to search their card and cross out the word/letter as appropriate. The children who are first to cross off all nine words or letters should shout 'BINGO'.

(**Marking ladder**)

Name: _____

Pupil	Objective	Teacher
	What could I do to improve my work next time?	

Classworks Literacy Year 1 © Louise Gilbert, Nelson Thornes Ltd 2003